FRONTIER EMERGING EQUITY MARKETS SECURITIES PRICE BEHAVIOR AND VALUATION

DATE DUE

FRONTIER EMERGING EQUITY MARKETS SECURITIES PRICE BEHAVIOR AND VALUATION

by

Oliver S. Kratz

KLUWER ACADEMIC PUBLISHERS
Boston / Dordrecht / London

Distributors for North, Central and South America:
Kluwer Academic Publishers
101 Philip Drive
Assinippi Park
Norwell, Massachusetts 02061 USA
Telephone (781) 871-6600
Fax (781) 871-6528
E-Mail <kluwer@wkap.com>

Distributors for all other countries:
Kluwer Academic Publishers Group
Distribution Centre
Post Office Box 322
3300 AH Dordrecht, THE NETHERLANDS
Telephone 31 78 6392 392
Fax 31 78 6546 474
E-Mail <services@wkap.nl>

 Electronic Services <http://www.wkap.nl>

Library of Congress Cataloging-in-Publication Data
Kratz, Oliver S., 1971-
    Frontier emerging equity markets securities price behavior and
valuation / by Oliver S. Kratz.
    p. cm.
  Includes bibliographical references and index.
  ISBN 0-7923-8585-3
  1. Securities--Prices--Russia (Federation) 2.
Stock-exchanges-- Russia (Federation) I. Title.
  HG5580.2.A3 K73 1999
  332.63'2'0947 -- dc21
                      99-33709
                      CIP

Printed on acid-free paper.
Printed in the United States of America

To
Leanna
and
Horst Kratz (1939-1989)

Contents

Foreword

Financial intermediation understood as the efficient channelling and allocation of surplus savings into productive investments is at the core of economic growth and yet continues in many developing countries to be overly dependent on commercial banks. In the last decade, transition economies have started to loosen the grip of their antiquated banking systems by nurturing the emergence of embryonic capital markets which have proven highly effective conduits for attracting foreign equity capital. The global financial crisis of the last two years however has shown that the compelling logic for forging ahead on the emergence path is fraught with trials and tribulations that such economies are often ill-equipped to cope with; fund managers – often at loss on how to gauge the risk/return matrix in such markets – do not fare better.

"Frontier Emerging Equity Markets Securities Price Behavior and Valuation" is a seminal study which provides an insightful conceptual framework to understand the price formation and the valuation of equities traded in the pre-emerging capital market of Russia. Scholars, capitalists and policy-makers alike will find Oliver Kratz' path-breaking empirical study of the Russian equity market to be a powerful proxy for understanding and investing in other emerging capital markets.

Laurent Jacque
Professor of International Banking and Finance
The Fletcher School of Law and Diplomacy

The economic crises of 1997-99, although fading, are a reminder that global flows of capital can do great damage when domestic financial and business institutions are not set up to use them well. One major lesson from these troubles is that short-term bank loans in foreign currencies can be very risky if they are large relative to other forms of finance. The safest, most stable, and arguably the most productive type of capital flow has been direct foreign investment, though even there, if the rules for investors create monopoly and protection, damage can be done. Flows of portfolio capital fall between the two. They are more stable than bank loans but less than direct investment. How can they play a stabilizing and constructive role in a nation's development? One way is to help create the institutions that create clarity, transparency, and efficient capital allocation.

This work is aimed at helping investors find a way to dip their toes into markets that are just getting started. As local businesses begin to appreciate the advantages of honest accounting and responding to shareholders, "smart" money will flow in and tend to be more stable than hot, speculative, and "dumb" capital flows. Firms that climb up the ladder of transparency will find financing easier. Unless the government and other local businesses are unwilling to allow these firms to emerge, and if they have the power to prevent their growth, they will eventually succeed. Thus, this book should be seen as one contributing to a more stable and efficient global capital market. If it is used successfully, it will also allow investors to make some extra returns without too much risk. The author is to be congratulated for tackling a tough problem with energy, intelligence, and tenacity. Emerging markets demand all these, and patience.

David Dapice,
Harvard Institute for International Development
Professor of Economics, Tufts University

Oliver Kratz's new book is an insightful and novel contribution to the study of a new asset class - frontier equity markets. The book is an essential read for investment professionals seeking more effective methods for analyzing and valuing pre-emerging markets. It also provides a comprehensive overview for the novice to the field of emerging markets, as well as to the policymaker looking to gain a better understanding of the dynamics of frontier markets. Using Russia as a case study, Dr. Kratz examines investors' approach to valuing Russian equities during the early development stage of the equity market. Dr. Kratz's analysis of the rapid ascension and subsequent collapse of the Russian market support his contention that conventional methods of valuation alone are inadequate when applied to frontier markets. He poses the question: How does one analyze the behavior of frontier markets and quantify them in an economic model? The novelty of Dr. Kratz's approach lies in blending conventional valuation methods with new frontier market custom-designed valuation tools. Dr. Kratz's W-A-M valuation model measures not only fundamental and technical criteria but also qualitative criteria in relation to the price performance of securities and thus covers the increasingly important dimension of investor sentiment.

This book finally offers the first hard empirical data on frontier markets and conclusions that provide new insight into pre-emerging market equities and their price behavior. The author's conclusions are certain to fuel the future debate on financial asset pricing for frontier equity markets.

Courtney Fellowes
Director, Emerging Markets
Merrill Lynch

Chapter 1

Introduction
The markets that came in from the cold

Throughout this decade, emerging markets have gained an increasingly visible role in international finance. The globalization of financial institutions and the dismantling of the Soviet Union have transformed many formerly centrally-planned economies into free markets with fledgling stock exchanges. Consequently, a rising number of foreign market participants has been attracted to the newest playground of global finance: frontier emerging equity markets, or simply, pre-emerging markets.

Emerging markets, as we know them in Latin American and Asia, are not new in investment portfolios. Latin American and Asian emerging markets have become core investments in many global portfolios throughout the past two decades. The same cannot be said about the less known and less liquid brethren of equity markets in emerging Europe, which only recently surfaced on the radar screen of active investment management professionals. There are many important differences between the more mature emerging markets and the new, or pre-emerging markets. One, and probably the most important difference in the larger context of this book is the characteristic that is responsible for many of the puzzling relationships in frontier market finance we are witnessing. Specifically, it is the rapid and unprecedented speed at which investment professionals embraced opportunities in frontier emerging equity markets, thus shortening the maturing process of those equity environments and fostering a culture of high rewards, higher risks, and unprecedented volatility – in most cases resulting from an untested investment approach.

The speed of investment decision-making partially helps to explain what really happened in the early and mid-1990s in many of the newly emerging markets. Without a doubt, it was not a sober investment process, but an exercise in indiscriminate credit dumping onto the 'brown fields' of the former communist world. Why did it happen so quickly and in such an oblivious manner? Some answers may suggest that the mid-1990s presented a unique time in global capital markets. Investors had become used to earning 20% and more on their traditional blue-chip developed market investments. At one point, the delicate balance between greed and fear was in an irreparable disequilibrium. More markets and more equities needed to be found that promised even better returns. This was the time when the markets of Eastern Europe and the former Soviet Union, particularly Russia, offered themselves conveniently for investment allocation. No single week passed without large mutual fund companies losing many of their best analysts to hedge funds investing in such frontier markets. The investment analysis process became careless and fund managers became complacent. Instant double-digit returns were taken for granted.

Nevertheless, the rally lasted for 900% or 1000% in many markets. Until the supply of new risk-seeking capital dried up. Many dedicated hedge funds were fully invested. Mutual funds did not waste much time and followed. With mutual funds entering the stage of exotic investing, the discipline of investment analysis and lengthy committee decision-making on asset allocation also re-entered the set of valuation parameters in these markets. Eventually, many of the frontier markets required re-justification for their valuation levels.

One of the more prominent cases exemplifying the excess liquidity in untested pre-emerging markets was given in a different part of the world. It is that of brokerages justifying the price/earnings levels of 40-50x of so-called Chinese 'red-chips' during mid-1997. These were Hong Kong-listed companies which derived most of their revenue from mainland China, and which are co-owned by government or quasi-government entities. Investment analysts needed to create a new way of justifying such exorbitant valuations. One of the terms which was coined during this time was the 'concept-premium.' This meant that certain 'red-chips' could justify outrageously high valuation levels if there was a chance that more businesses would be acquired at politically negotiated 'bargain prices', and thus would become highly accretive to earnings.

Justification and interpretation of criteria factoring into valuation of frontier market securities is the underlying leitmotif in this book. This book examines the process of frontier market investing and points out the usual suspects and common pitfalls. We now know the repercussions of what can happen if conventional analysis fails. For the first time, we have barely enough data to make some statements with external validity in a statistical context. Also, for the first time, frontier markets such as Russia have become more than a conversational topic of adventurers and extreme-value fund managers, or highly speculative investments outfits.

During 1998 and 1999, the world was witnessing how its premier financial institutions reported losses and its best and brightest financial practitioners were left on the losing side of the investment game called Russia. Russia, once a frontier market, and again a frontier market, has impacted the global economy much beyond the size of its GDP could ever explain. Russian GKO defaults have led to top credit spread widening, and to a credit crunch for an infinite number of borrowers in less secure macro-economic environments. Understanding the dynamics of frontier markets, thus, becomes imperative to any student and practitioner of international finance.

In 1996, the Russian equity market was the best performing market in the world. In the twelve months period between August 1997 and August 1998, the Russian equity market became the worst performing market in the world. During the first two months of 1999, the Russian market again became the best performing equity market in the world. As such, the Russian case study offers a multitude of unique insights into a new sub-discipline of financial markets and security analysis: pre-emerging market securities price behavior and valuation.

The overarching theme of this book is pre-emerging market equity analysis – a sub-discipline which yet stands to be offered formal admission into conventional academic thinking in the field of financial markets. This book attempts to marry conventional empirical work on emerging market analysis and securities price behavior with a number of new intellectual territories that are proprietary to the unique circumstances of frontier emerging equity markets and their main set of actors. The lessons that can be learnt from the rapidly emerging Russian equity market and its subsequent virtual collapse are numerous. This book develops an analytical framework for understanding how pre-emerging equity markets are created, how they can be more efficiently analyzed with a set of new valuation tools, and how the same features, which generate quick returns, can lead to an explosive set of circumstances and equity market characteristics, that can draw the map for financial meltdown. The repercussions are often felt in not only equity portfolios but in shifting geopolitical landscapes and civil unrest, thus raising the relevance of understanding the complex mechanisms driving pre-emerging markets beyond the simple measurement of profits and losses in investment portfolios.

The performance of the Russian equity market since the inception of the Russian Trading System (RTS) in September 1995, has attracted awareness not only from hedge funds and fairly dedicated emerging markets institutional investors, but also increasingly from mainstream international mutual funds. With the Russian equity market's movement to one of the center stages of emerging market equity investment and its eventual inclusion in the major emerging market indices, the Russian equity market had also become the focus of attention at an increasing number of Russia-dedicated equity conferences in New York, London, Moscow, and some of the off-shore investment bases during 1996. The discussions that have arisen at many conferences, in the global asset management departments of institutional money managers, and in classrooms preparing students for financial analysis, have and still revolve around the questions of how really to analyze the behavior of pre-emerging market equities for valuation purposes and timely investment.

Traditional fundamental analysis, ratio analysis or 'mining' for cash flow data seem justifiably not the right method in an environment where financial statements initially have not been available or frequently are only available in local accounting standards which often bear few similarities with US G.A.A.P. or International Accounting Standards (IAS). For many of the companies, management was, and sometimes still is, reluctant to provide useful and audited information regarding their assets, operations, ownership structure, liabilities, barter agreements, or simply more detail about the often convoluted political-private ownership web of relationships steering the future strategy of a company. The most telling occurrence, that all equity analysts of Russian securities will recall, is when again one of the blue-chip Wall Street brokerages' earnings estimates of Russian companies deviated 50% or more from the actual reported earnings number.[1] This, however, has been the environment in which analysts of Russian securities have been working, and in which the question of how to separate the winners from the

---

[1] Merrill Lynch reports on August 27th, 1997 in the weekly Russia comment that a survey of US investment institutions found:
1. Nearly 90% of respondents said Russian companies failed to provide adequate financial, operational and strategic information to shareholders.
2. Nearly 70% said that government attempts to enforce shareholder-friendly legislation were only 'fair to poor'.
3. More than 80% of investors said that they expected to maintain or increase exposure to Russia over the next twelve months.

losers in a pre-emerging equity universe has become the topic of choice among market participants.

As chart 1.0. depicts, not only have brokerages malfunctioned in forecasting actual earnings, but even more interestingly, they have not remotely reached a consensus when deriving their estimates. An average deviation of +/-65% from mean forecasts indicates that sell-side research analysts are either not working under the same assumptions or that pre-emerging market companies inform securities analysts poorly.

Chart 1.0. 1996 Brokerage EPS estimates dispersion of Russian equities

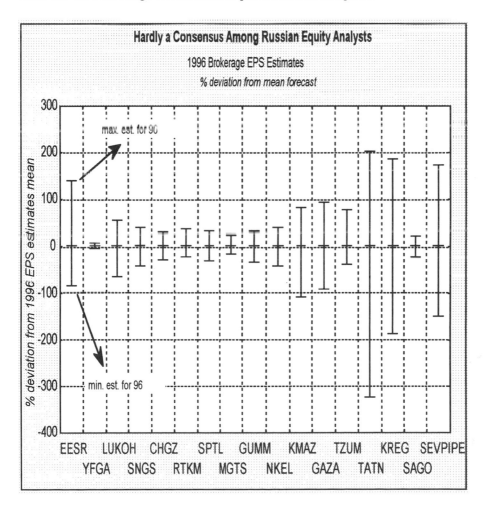

6 *Chapter 1*

The first view could be supported by the fact that many research analysts assessing pre-emerging market companies lack the experience to derive meaningful assumptions. This phenomenon is not unusual for a number of newly emerging markets where the lack of experts in such markets and countries, forces brokerages to fill sell-side research analyst positions with recent graduates who sometimes happen to speak the particular local language. The other view, that firms in pre-emerging equity markets seem to less than adequately address securities analysts' quantitative inquiries, however, appears to be more plausible. In either case, buy-side analysts and portfolio managers are often presented with a melange of different estimates and hence cannot deduce much meaning from any of them.

Chart 1.1. I/B/E/S EPS estimates for other emerging market blue chips and US blue chips

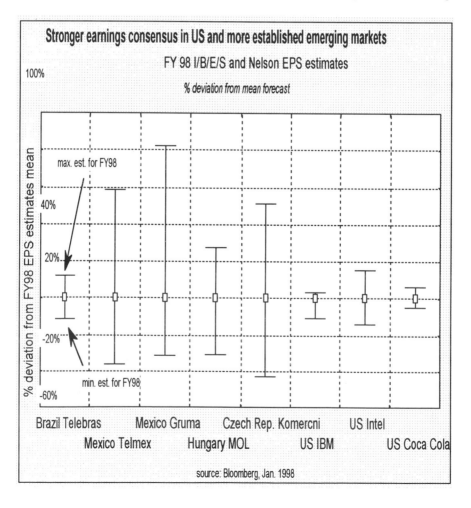

In chart 1.1., which has been added to demonstrate the deviation from mean earnings estimates for some blue-chip equities in Brazil, Mexico, Czech Republic and Hungary, and finally some US technology and food sector stocks, it becomes apparent that the Russian blue-chips, depicted in chart 1.0., have higher deviations from their mean estimates than those blue-chips in more established Central European and Latin American markets. Particularly noteworthy is the realization that U.S. technology stocks, which are often referred to as volatile, or speculative investments, enjoy dramatically lower dispersion in their earnings estimates than the Russia sample in chart 1.0. Given the degree of information scarcity and insufficient data quality in frontier markets, a need to become more imaginative and to apply valuation metrics reaching beyond financials-based measures has emerged when assessing equities in Russia - as well as in those frontier markets which are to emerge in Ukraine, Romania, Bulgaria and the Central Asian republics. This book focuses on such methods which, on the basis of generally available information, can create a new insight into the price behavior of pre-emerging market equities maturing from their infant stages to well-researched, transparent, and sufficiently liquid equities.

While recognizing that the Russian equity market has made substantial progress in its development and that companies which manage their investor relations well and release reliable financial statements indeed exist, it is obvious that these firms still form a minority. In the beginning, before three digit returns were recorded, and before Russia sub-merged into complete financial meltdown, those companies virtually did not exist.

In this context, the following chapters shall primarily shed light upon the phase of rapid financial emergence when Russia was still referred to as the Wild East and the country of Robber Baron Capitalism – or maybe infant capitalism. All credit is given to those champions of transparency that have most recently allowed the first full Economic Value Added (EVA) analysis on their enterprises and fashion multimedia presentations at investor conferences in New York and London. In this sense, one should not forget to pay tacit homage to the progress that has been made by the very few companies since 1994.

The usefulness of the analytical frameworks presented in this book, however, must be in their application to frontier markets that are yet to emerge in Central Asia, Eastern Europe and sub-Saharan Africa, and re-emerge in Russia.

Given the progress that had been made, and that had been responsible for Russia's inclusion into every international investment portfolio, it must be noted that Russia –even before the financial meltdown of 1998-   still remained a pre-emerging or frontier market in many ways. There are few other markets in which some of the largest enterprises, such as gigantic engineering firms (Uralmash or Izhorsky Zavod), or the world's largest cargo-aircraft manufacturer (Aviastar) were considered second-, or even third-tier stocks.

There are arguably a number of approaches to find clarification for some of the thoughts and questions that have been evoked during the past two years, as pre-emerging equity analysts and policy makers have grappled with the many issues pertaining to security valuation or administration of new securities exchanges. The path chosen in this book appears to be the most intuitive. It takes the reader from a basic introduction to the Russian pre-emerging market, to a more elaborate and formalized analysis of securities price behavior in the context of market efficiency. It finally culminates in a dynamic valuation model for pre-emerging equity markets and offers a number of explanatory frameworks for the sudden collapse of many pre-emerging markets, such as Russia in 1998, or Romania and Ukraine in 1997.

Besides offering an educational journey on pre-emerging markets for the student of financial markets, this book develops analytical frameworks for the emerging markets professional to answer the following two questions: Firstly, how can the returns process of pre-emerging market securities be characterized in econometric modeling terms in the context of market efficiency?   Secondly, how can the emerging market portfolio manager assess frontier market equities in the attempt to mine for data, which would result in future outperformance?   The first question of evolving relative market efficiency is tied to the latter by the notion of relative market inefficiency being possibly responsible for the erratic behavior of securities which attract investors despite the lack of reliable data.

If a dynamic process from relative market inefficiency to relative market efficiency can be measured, it could be presumed that the market was 'stacked' against outsiders. If this were the case, it would be at least important to know.   More importantly, however, knowledge about the relative efficiency or relative inefficiency of the pre-emerging equity market would shed light upon the frequently cited notion that inefficiency is less desirable from a policy standpoint as investment is commonly said to shun inefficient markets and thus not fuel the real economy with capital - and such investments that are made are poorly allocated.   Under such circumstances, the economic efficiency of the financial intermediation process (which allocates savings to investments) would be impaired. Furthermore, the exploration of informational efficiency or inefficiency may help the portfolio investor to understand this market and generate ideas for exploiting inefficiencies in this market, or any other market with similar characteristics. To round up the exploration of informational efficiency in the Russian equity market, the extent to which market efficiency is a function of securities transparency, will also be assessed

Diagram 1.0. Exploratory diagram of causal factor of relative market efficiency

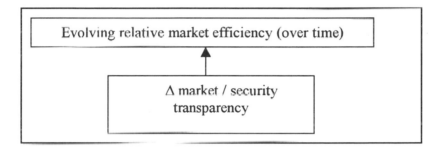

The attempt to attribute the changing degree of market efficiency to those factors that are believed to increase the appeal of securities to investors could create a new paradigm for policy makers in frontier markets to think about the various development paths of their capital markets in a more targeted and market efficiency-oriented fashion (i.e. if transparency is a factor contributing to market efficiency and market efficiency leads to a lower risk perception and thus higher investment, then transparency itself should be targeted as one of the first statutes to be implemented by any securities exchange commission). This argument is based on the premise that improving relative market efficiency helps the development of an emerging equity market. To support this premise, one must agree on the benefits of having an emerging equity market over not having an equity market, and instead relying solely on a banking system for the financial intermediation process of allocating capital between savers and investors. The benefits of an emerging equity market are briefly outlined in table 1.0.

Table 1.0. Benefits of an emerging equity market

• **mobilization** of domestic investors' savings – enhanced set of financial instruments are available to savers • **source of investment capital at relatively low cost** • **equity can be better than debt** – company less vulnerable to fluctuations in earnings; company less vulnerable to interest rate increases • **more efficient allocation of capital** – near continuous valuation of share price – shareholder can effect changes in mgmt. of quoted companies, therefore managerial resources are allocated more efficiently – foreign equity inflows provide host nation with foreign corporate finance expertise • **from a global perspective:** -capital is channeled to the countries with the highest risk-adjusted returns which translates into a net gain for the global economy

The last three chapters of this book are dedicated to detecting measures, events and characteristics of equities that fill the void of more conventional information when analyzing securities. In particular, transparency and liquidity-enhancement programs are explored. The results create a new insight into pre-emerging market equities and their likely future performance in an environment where such measures remain only second best tools, albeit, in the absence of better ones.

Diagram 1.1. Exploration of factors contributing to outperformance of securities in frontier equity markets

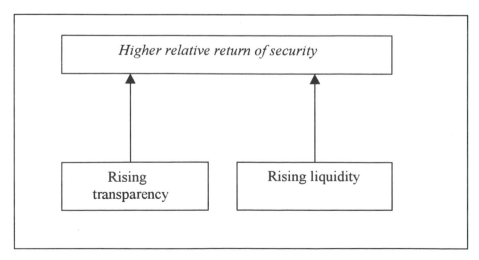

The results presented in the last three chapters of this book also suggest ways of further examining the factors that contribute to companies' decisions to apply for American depository receipt programs (ADRs) or those factors which cause brokerages to initiate continuous coverage of specific firms. Primarily, the last three chapters develop a dynamic framework of equity valuation in pre-emerging markets. This goal is achieved by measuring fundamental and technical / qualitative criteria in relation to securities price performance, assessing the virtues and vices of depository receipt programs, and finally exploring the philology of frontier markets valuation.

In a broader context, this book has immediate relevance for two personae: the policy maker seeking means to nurture the financial intermediation process, and the student of security analysis, seeking ways to assess securities that lack the beneficial membership of the I/B/E/S (International Brokerage Estimates Survey) database and all the transparency features and estimates that would result from it. In a broader sense, this book serves those willing to explore frontier equity markets with a framework based on market segmentation theory and behavioral finance.

Diagram 1.2. Beneficiaries of analysis

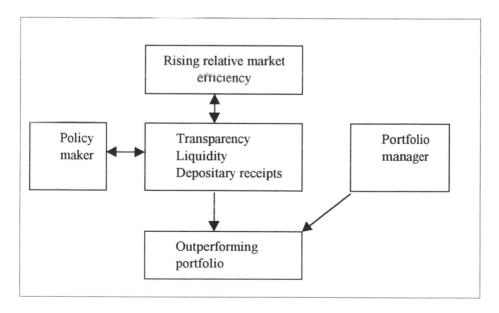

On a third level, this book also highlights some subtle points that have been observed: Pre-emerging market securities are assessed by blending the investment community's assumptions of a country, which are often tied to a large portion of goodwill and optimism generated by the general media, and the political bias the country carries. In this sense, it is not a surprise that investors fully embraced the Russian equity market. It marked a historical event finally culminating in the conversion of the other Cold War power to a rogue form of dilettantish Capitalism.

The best example that comes to mind is the issuance of the Russian Federation's first Eurobond (1996) since the fall of the Russian Czar (1917). The oversubscription of the issue and the 'historical' event of the Russian government coming to New York in October 1996, bore more resemblance to a grandiose diplomatic event than a shrewd question and answer session probing the creditworthiness of the borrower. Equities such as Gazprom, the giant hydro-carbon conglomerate, are perceived with a similar bias, which more often than not benefits the company and leaves traditional investment analysis marginalized on the sidelines. This was the first touch of irrational exuberance spelling disaster in faint letters and hinting at the future collapse of the Russian financial system.

While this book will largely abstain from exploring this third notion of intangible country bias accompanying valuation of equity markets, it may be important to keep at least in mind. The only numerical mention of this notion can be found in the analysis of the meaning of the Russian Eurobond spread in the context of the Russian equity market performance, a section which can be found in chapter 9. Obviously, political biases will vary by country and be determined by size, history, and related variables. Despite parallels that may be drawn from the results, the difference between Russia, China, and smaller emerging equity markets will also be a function of their political past and thus may not be the best example for the behavior of security prices of smaller markets with less research coverage or negligible past impact on global politics and economics.

As this third notion will not be the core of the analysis, it is examined only in a cursory fashion. Where appropriate, some elements worthy mentioning are presented, primarily in the context of some new theories of behavioral finance – a topic which overlaps with the notion of market efficiency and thus will not derail the main theme of this book from its two primary objectives.

I.A. Preview by chapter

Chapter 2 introduces the reader to the overall framework of securities price behavior by outlining the major premises of the efficient market hypothesis. From there, the most current empirical results of developed markets are discussed. The nexus between securities behavior in developed markets and securities behavior in emerging markets is established via a brief assessment of the meaning of relative market efficiency and the utility of tests of absolute market efficiency versus relative market efficiency. The final section of chapter 2 provides numerous examples of recent empirical work on emerging market securities behavior in the context of market efficiency. Chapter 2 concludes by noting some of the newer, behavioral finance-based explanations for less than perfectly efficient markets.

Chapter 3 develops a framework for the genesis of a pre-emerging equity market using Russia as a case study. Subsequently, issues such as market regulation, clearing and settlement, custody, the creation of the Russian Trading System (RTS), taxation and offshore investing, Russian accounting peculiarities, and the often ignored connection between equity market infrastructure and equity valuation, are explored. Overall, chapter 3 helps to gain an insight into the unique characteristics of a young emerging equity market. It highlights the main problems and points out the areas where progress has been achieved. Furthermore, continuous reference to websites helps the reader to retrieve current updates on many of the pre-emerging market developments addressed. The goal of chapter 3, is to establish an understanding of topics in equity market infrastructure. Above all, equity market infrastructure serves as a valuation benchmark for the companies that are located in a specific market. The example of Russia demonstrates that no single company valuation can be isolated from the risks of the equity market infrastructure in Russia. The deficiencies in the infrastructure of the Russian equity market are one of the main structural reasons why a steep discount to Russia's companies versus their peers in more mature emerging market continues to exist.

In Chapter 4, a more quantitative framework is presented in order to demonstrate some of the data peculiarities of the Russian pre-emerging market. The main financial statistics, such as Sharpe ratio, skewness, kurtosis, mean, standard deviation and normality tests are computed and their relevance is brought into context. In addition, the mean-variance frontier is plotted for three distinct time periods covering the rapid primary emergence process. It becomes apparent that the traditional risk-return trade-off relationship does not hold in the early stages of frontier emerging markets, but is increasingly developing at a later stage. Given the relative neglect of volatility as a measure to trade-off return, it can be concluded that pre-emerging market investors are initially less concerned about volatility than about more fundamental risks – a notion which any frontier market investment professional will easily confirm. Furthermore, the underlying probability distribution demonstrates clear deviation from normality. This realization gives rise to a search for methodologies that are robust to non-normality and heteroscedasticity.

Chapter 5, in many ways, delivers a novel approach to pre-emerging markets analysis. Here the reader is introduced to the information channels which serve pre-emerging market investors in their decision-making process. The investor in the Russian equity market uses brokerage reports as the most important source of information. Ranking below brokerage reports are several on-line services, newspapers and magazines. The transparency index, which builds the core of the chapter is established by tracking brokerage coverage of individual companies in the Russian equity market, which then are categorized into top-, medium-, and bottom-transparency portfolios. The overarching theme of informational efficiency finds its closest description in this chapter and lays the groundwork for the analytical assessment of relative market efficiency in chapter 7.

In Chapter 6, the methodology for measuring relative market efficiency in emerging markets is established. The chapter begins by explaining the linkage between the random walk model and the efficient market hypothesis. Subsequently, the technical assumptions of the variance ratio test, which serves to test the random walk model, are developed. Several econometric parts, not vital to the understanding of the general ideas, enhance the tool set for students and quantitative practitioners of pre-emerging market asset analysis.

Chapter 7 applies the variance ratio test to three portfolios of Russian equities formed according to the transparency criteria laid out in chapter 5. The empirical results indicate that low- and high-transparency portfolios suffer from a similar degree of relative market inefficiency, whereas the medium-transparency portfolio displays a higher degree of relative market efficiency. The underlying reasons for this phenomenon are mainly related to poor information dissemination (bottom-transparency portfolio), non-dedicated investor participation, institutional characteristics that lead to buy-and-hold strategy (top-transparency portfolio), and dedicated country and emerging market funds composing the investor pool in the medium-transparency portfolio. In the second section of chapter 7, evolving relative market efficiency of the Russian index over time is examined. Here one can see a trend that indicates increasing relative market efficiency. This trend tends to be interrupted during times of market corrections following market rallies. The reason for such lapses into relative market inefficiency are mainly found in the inadequate infrastructure of the Russian equity market, which excludes smaller brokerages, due to counterparty risk considerations, during times of market correction. This is primarily the result of a lack of a central clearing mechanism. This chapter explores the basic assumption that informational efficiency fostered by securities transparency, eventually translates into a higher degree of relative market efficiency. This assumption is qualified as a severe form of market segmentation, and introduces some initially counterintuitive findings. These findings demonstrate that relative market efficiency is assaulted as dominating forces related to a special segment of investors in the top transparency portfolio defeat the mechanism that translates higher transparency into a higher degree of relative market efficiency. This finding opens the search for many potentially profitable investment strategies.

Chapter 8 begins by introducing international depository receipt programs to the reader. The main benefits to the issuer and to the investor are outlined. Further, the four different types of depository receipts facilities are explained. Following this introduction, depository programs issued by Russian companies are examined. Other facets of Russian depository receipts, issues such as ADR arbitrage, trading trends in underlying shares with ADRs, and the case study of the Gazprom ringfence assault attempt, are addressed. Finally, the chapter takes a closer analytical look at the performance of underlying shares pre- and post-issuance of depository receipts, thus adding and denying evidence to many myths pertaining to the investment in underlying shares around the issuance date of depository receipts.

Depository receipt programs have become the most popular and widespread means for emerging market companies in their attempt to close the valuation gap between developing and developed markets. Further, they have become a conduit for many asset managers and retail investors to participate in emerging markets without the implied custody and settlement risk associated with inadequate securities infrastructure in emerging markets. Chapter 8 takes a critical look at the benefits and costs created by depository receipt programs with special attention paid to the crucial valuation dimension affecting underlying shares in local market trading.

Chapter 9 carries the analysis of equities in the Russian pre-emerging equity market a step further by developing a transparency-dynamic equity valuation model. This model, which is based on market segmentation theory, develops a framework for the investor to decide when to rely on the WAM factor (Western Auditor-ADR-Market Capitalization), and when to switch to fundamental ratios when assessing the future performance of pre-emerging markets. The chapter rounds up the discussion by presenting a simple reference framework for screening pre-emerging market equities in the context of political, macro-economic, equity infrastructure, and WAM/fundamental factors.

In chapter 10, a new framework for understanding the equity return and information relationship in frontier equity markets is presented. This framework draws on Aristotle's philosophy of rhetoric and Richard Dawkins' theory of memes. The interdependence of rapid emergence and sudden financial collapse is explored. The notion of market sentiment affecting equity prices is incorporated into the pre-emerging equity market screening framework. This marries empirical work rooted in the halls of academe with the most recent experience of practitioners on Wall Street and global asset management departments investing in such markets. Moreover, it touches upon one of the newer paradigms in frontier emerging market investment management: the multi-layered effects of economic linkage, sentiment linkage, and finally philological linkage, as the accelerating reinforcing mechanism in the vicious and virtuous cycles of frontier emerging market price behavior. The chapter closes by suggesting a way of how to become an astute investor in frontier equity markets, and how to time investment decisions in a profitable and sensible way.

Chapter 2

Market Efficiency in Frontier Emerging Markets
Prelude to a hypothetical journey

In the context of this book the concept of market efficiency becomes relevant as it lends itself as a framework to examine the behavior of securities returns on a level which is of interest to the portfolio manager, whose mandate it is to outperform a benchmark, and who can profit from or exploit gross market inefficiencies. Secondly, it is important to the policy maker, whose mandate it is to steer and control the development of a newly emerging market in order to achieve the benefits of an efficient equity market.

The concept of an efficient market differs from the economic notion of a perfect market in which perfect information exchange, no transaction costs, and perfect trading infrastructure are assumed. The model of an efficient market does neither require rational behavior in an absolute sense of the word, nor does it require information to be perfect and always accurately reflected, although in the long run reality should reassert itself. There may, however, be times when investors collectively assess assets to be worth more than their intrinsic value. The major difference between the economic notion of a perfect market and the model which has become known among financial economists as the efficient market hypothesis (EMH) therefore is the relaxation of the assumption of perfection.

In simple words, financial markets are considered to display a form of relative efficiency if market participants are operating under the condition of a fair game where no single investor has a chance of beating her fellow investors in any consistent fashion, and not only under those circumstances when zero transaction costs are assumed and information is understood to be disseminated instantaneously and ubiquitously to all market participants.

Market efficiency also becomes an important concept in this book as its characteristics can be closely linked to the phenomenon of market segmentation, which forms one of the overarching themes of pre-emerging market behavior and thinking, and of the individual analyses presented throughout the following chapters. Market segmentation appears to be a controlling factor in determining relative market efficiency of securities with different characteristics, particularly in an environment where 'noise traders' or derivatives thereof may be predominant in securities with certain shared characteristics, or when liquidity constraints distort other valuation parameters.

This chapter begins by outlining the concept of market efficiency and its major underlying assumptions. The linkage between the concept of market efficiency and the random walk model, which is used in many econometric tests as a tool to *measure* market efficiency, is described in detail in a later section of this book and thus a more disciplined inquiry into the linkage will be postponed at this point.[1]

Following the general framework of market efficiency, an overview of recent empirical results on developed markets is presented. Particularly, results from two popular methods: autocorrelations and variance ratio tests are discussed. Finally, an overview of selected relevant methodologies and of previous studies covering the special cases of emerging equity markets is presented. The chapter concludes by briefly describing some theories derived from behavioral finance and their effect on efficiency in emerging markets.

II.A. Market efficiency

II.A.1. Market efficiency in developed markets

Market efficiency has been one of the most widely discussed issues in finance and as such it shall be briefly defined before proceeding to the more

---

[1] The term to *measure* is deliberately used as preference over to *test* market efficiency. Measuring market efficiency implies a relative degree as opposed to testing market efficiency, which implies an absolute degree of market efficiency or inefficiency.

immediately relevant subject of the random walk theory. There are five key assumption which underlie the efficient market hypothesis (EMH)[2]:

1. A large number of rational, profit-maximizing investors who actively participate in the market by analyzing, valuing, and trading stocks
2. Price-taking behavior
3. Information is free and dispersed to market participants at the same time Information is generated randomly; that is announcements are essentially independent of one another
4. Investors react quickly and accurately to new information, causing stock prices to adjust accordingly

As we will later see, these assumptions leave substantial room for subjective interpretation. Indeed, there are tests of market efficiency that discredit market efficiency in developed markets on the grounds of non-fulfillment of the assumptions laid out above. Generally, the usefulness of such logical scrutiny of the premises on which the efficient market hypothesis is founded, delivers fairly subjective, mildly academically relevant, but practically inconsequential results. As such, those shall not be the focus of this chapter. Nevertheless, as we will see in the example of a study on the Polish equity market described below, the violation of the five assumption can hint at results that can also be proven quantitatively.

The three commonly discussed forms of the efficient market hypothesis (EMH) have been defined as follows:

Table 2.0. Three Forms of Market Efficiency

Traditional three forms of market efficiency
Weak Form Efficient Market Hypothesis: Stock prices are assumed to reflect all information that is contained in past history of the share price itself.
Semi-strong Form of Efficient Market Hypothesis: All publicly available information such as financial statements, strategy, past history, etc. is reflected in current share price.
Strong Form of Efficient Market Hypothesis: All public and private information is reflected in the current share price.[3]

---

[2] Charles P. Jones, *Investments: Analysis and Management*, 3rd ed., (New York: John Wiley & Sons, Inc.), 464.

[3] For a detailed description of the three forms of the market efficiency see E.F. Fama, "Efficient Capital Markets: Review of Theoretical and Empirical Work," *Journal of Finance* (May 1970): 383-417.

The relationship among the informational sets described in table 2.0. can be graphically illustrated in diagram 2.0.

Diagram 2.0. Efficient Market Hypothesis

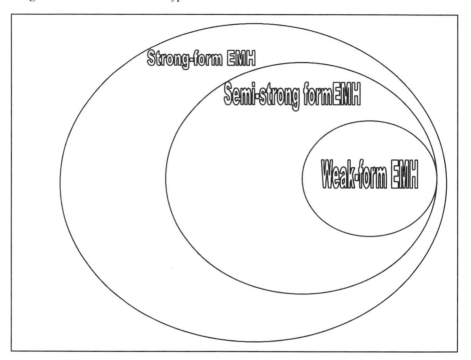

In technical terms the relationship can be defined as:

WF EMH= weak form EMH

SSF EMH= semi-strong form EMH

SF EMH= strong form EMH

WF EMH ⊂ SSF EMH and SSF EMH ⊂ SF EMH,

where all information contained in WF EMH is also contained in SSF EMH, but SSF EMH is superior because is contains some additional information, and all information of SSF EMH is contained in SF EMH, but SF EMH is superior because it contains some additional information.

The validity of the weak form EMH would render all technical and chartist efforts meaningless as they solely rely on the past behavior of securities prices. The validity of the semi-strong form of EMH would question not only the technician's but also the fundamental securities analyst's value-added as fundamental analysis based on publicly available information (private information would be considered insider trading) would not create excess return over any sustainable period of time. Finally, the implications of the strong form EMH would leave no one with a way to beat the market. Thus, many financial decisions or other actions would perfectly lose their meaning. Share buy-backs based on the company's 'insider' view that the stock price is undervalued, for example, would therefore not be justified.[4]

For each of the three forms of EMH, a number of methods have been devised to measure the validity of the respective forms of the market efficiency hypothesis:[5]

Table 2.1. Common measurement methodologies associated with EMH

Weak form EMH	*Semi-strong form EMH*	*Strong from EMH*
Autocorrelation	Event study tests focusing on:	Examining the performance of alternative investor groups,
Runs Test	Stock splits, earnings estimates, new issues, size effects, calendar	such as corporate insiders, stock exchange specialists,
Filter Rules	effects.	professional money managers.

The weak form of the EMH is also associated with the random walk theory or hypothesis. The random walk hypothesis states that successive price changes or successive rates of return of a security are independent over time and that the actual price or return fluctuates around an intrinsic, or a theoretical value. Fama, the pioneer of efficient market theory, remarks in this context:

---

[4] Share buy-backs in order to gain ownership share or to benefit from favorable tax treatment would be justified under the strong-form EMH.
[5] For a detailed discussion of empirical findings of EMH tests of developed markets refer to Frank K. Reilly, *Investment Analysis and Portfolio Management*, 3rd edition, (Fort Worth: The Dryden Press, 1989), chap. 6 passim.

"...the theory of random walks implies that a series of stock price changes has no memory -the past history of a series cannot be used to predict the future in any meaningful way. The future path of the price level of a security is no more predictable than the path of a series of accumulated random numbers."[6]

Furthermore, Fama notes that market efficiency and asset pricing models are inseparably joint-hypotheses and therefore are not testable. This would imply that existing return predictability would not necessarily establish market inefficiency, but could be the result of a joint-hypothesis problem. Given this argumentation, which is based on the premise that any discovered inefficiency may be the result of analysts using the wrong pricing model or possibly the wrong reference benchmark for the measurement of abnormal returns, it would almost lead to the conclusion that any study including measures of market efficiency would lead to questionable results. This theoretical debate, however, has not found its last answer and as such most researchers, particularly those preoccupied with emerging capital markets, have abandoned this notion, and have continued to conduct tests of market efficiency. The prevailing view must be that only relative efficiency can be measured and improvements or deterioration in the serial dependence of assets prices would still be the strongest evidence of improving or deteriorating relative market efficiency.

II.A.2. Empirical results in developed markets

The main concern of empirical research in the area of market efficiency has been to prove the hypothesis of the random walk model which states that

---

[6] Eugene F. Fama, "Random Walk in Stock Market Prices," *Financial Analysts Journal* (Sept./Oct. 1965):56. Since Fama's classical definition, there have been iterations of this definition. A notable recent definition has been presented by Malkiel (1992): "A capital market is said to be efficient if it fully and correctly reflects all relevant information in determining security prices. Formally, the market is said to be efficient with respect to some information set...if security prices would be unaffected by revealing that information to all participants. Moreover, efficiency with respect to an information set...implies that it is impossible to make economic profits by trading on the basis of [that information set]." This definition includes the notion of economic gains and therefore emphasizes the difference between 'the perfect market' and 'efficient market in financial economics' where reality can be distorted as long as participants are collectively unaware of some additional information which would lead to a different valuation, and as long as no one possesses information beyond the defined information set which would allow for a trading strategy leading to economic gains.

successive price changes are independent. Most tests fall in one of two categories. The first one relies on statistical tools such as serial correlation, or more precisely, autocorrelations and non-parametric runs tests. If such tests support the independence of price changes, one would infer that no mechanical trading rules or chartist techniques would yield excess returns. It would imply that the market has no memory and historical patterns of price changes do not repeat themselves in any consistent fashion. The second category of tests has concentrated on testing independence by applying different trading rules and monitoring whether greater profits can be reached than through a simple buy-and-hold strategy.

Predictability in equity prices has been a broadly and continuously researched topic. It is impossible to provide a full survey of the extensive literature that has been produced over the years.[7] Therefore, and for the sake of relevance and currency of data, some of the most recent empirical evidence shall serve as a good indicator of what results have been achieved by applying autocorrelation tests and variance ratio tests in developed markets.[8] Campbell, Lo, and MacKinlay's recent work *The Econometrics of Financial Markets* (1997) includes the below described empirical results for two popular tests applied to the CRSP (Center for Research in Securities Prices at the University of Chicago) data series.[9] There are a number of other tests ranging from excess volatility-based tests to probability models for stock market crashes following the creation of bubbles. The final focus on pre-emerging markets in this book does not lend itself to tests that depend on analyses of dividend streams, which are components of an equilibrium model used and thus are mostly not applicable in a pre-emerging market environment where equilibrium models such as the CAPM have been proven not representative given the less than perfect integration in global capital markets.

Literature that attempts to discover causal relationships between security characteristics or market infrastructure and relative market efficiency has

---

[7] For a good review of the literature on EMH in developed markets, and particularly for a good description of excess volatility-based tests, and probability models for stock crashes based on bubble creation which would defeat the EMH also refer to Peter Fortune, "Stock Market Efficiency: An Autopsy?" *New England Economic Review-Federal Reserve Bank of Boston,*(March/April 1991): 17-40.

[8] The recent literature has been built on the works which include: Alexander (1961, 1964), Cootner (1964), Cowles (1960), Cowles and Jones (1937), Fama (1965), Fama and Blume (1966), Kendall (1953), Granger and Morgenstern (1963), Mandelbrot (1963), Osborne (1959, 1962), Roberts (1959), and Working (1960).

[9] John Y. Campbell, Andrew W. Lo, and A. Craig MacKinlay, *Econometrics of Financial Markets* (Princeton, N.J. Princeton University Press: 1997): 66-74.

been scarce and inconclusive at best. There is, however, a growing body of literature dealing with reasons why markets may not be efficient.[10] Most of the reasoning is based on theories in the relatively unexplored field of behavioral finance. Additional reasoning on the causes of market inefficiency is derived from market segmentation theory and models of noise trading.[11]

II.A.2.1. Tests of autocorrelation in developed markets

Table 2.2. reports the autocorrelation for both the value- and the equal-weighted CRSP index. The CRSP daily return index is measured by mean return, standard deviation, and 1-4 day lag autocorrelation coefficients. Subsequently the Box-Pierce Q-statistic is computed, which tests the joint-significance of the four autocorrelation measures. The results indicate that both the value- and the equal-weighted index have statistically significant positive serial correlations at the first lag. The Box-Pierce joint-significance test at five autocorrelations has a value of 263.3 which indicates significance at all conventional significance levels.[12] Interestingly, the autocorrelations in the first measurement interval between 1962 and 1978 are both, in the value- and in the equal-weighted index, substantially higher than in the second measurement period ranging from 1978 to 1994. The authors of this most recent study attribute this to the notion that predictability has been a 'source' of excess profits and thus its decline is consistent with increasingly competitive financial markets. These results suggest that more work can be done on the changing nature of market efficiency as expressed by declining and rising autocorrelation coefficients, particularly on the individual security level, as opposed to the aggregate index level.

---

[10] For a comprehensive summary of behavioral finance-based reasoning for market inefficiencies see Richard H. Thaler et al., eds., *Advances in Behavioral Finance*, (New York: Russell Sage Foundation, 1993).

[11] Peter Fortune, "Stock Market Efficiency: An Autopsy?," *New England Economic Review-Federal Reserve Bank of Boston*, (March/April 1991): 30-34. For a more detailed discussion of noise traders in the context of market segmentation theory please refer to chapter 7.

See also: Andrei Shleifer and Lawrence H. Summers, "The Noise Trader Approach in Finance," *Journal of Economic Perspectives*, (Spring 1990): 19-33.

Delong, J. Bradford; Andrei Shleifer; Lawrence H. Summers and Robert J. Waldmann. "Noise Trader Risk in Financial Markets." *Journal of Political Economy* (August 1990): 703-738.

[12] The Q-statistic is distributed asymptotically as an x^2-variate (5) for which the 99.5-percentile is 16.7.

Table 2.2. Empirical autocorrelation results of developed markets

Sample Period	Sample Size	Mean	SD	ρ1	ρ2	ρ3	ρ4	Q5	Q10
A. Daily Returns		**CRSP Value-Weighted Index**							
62:07:03-94:12:30	8179	0.041	0.824	17.6	-0.7	0.1	-0.8	263.3	269.5
62:07:03-78:10:27	4090	0.028	0.738	27.8	1.2	4.6	3.3	329.4	343.5
78:10:30-94:12:30	4089	0.054	0.901	10.8	-2.2	-2.9	-3.5	69.5	72.1
B. Daily Returns		**CRSP Equal Weighted Index**							
62:07:10-94:12:30	8179	0.07	0.764	35.0	9.3	8.5	9.9	1301.9	1369.5
62:07:03-78:10:27	4090	0.063	0.771	43.1	13.0	15.3	15.2	1062.2	1110.2
78:10:30-94:12:30	4089	0.078	0.756	26.2	4.9	2.0	4.9	348.9	379.5

II.A.2.2. Variance ratio tests in developed markets

The variance ratio test, which is described in detail in chapter 6, has been used to compute the results presented in table 2.3. As described in table 2.3., the data set and the measurement time periods are identical to those used in the above described autocorrelation test results.[13] The results largely confirm those of the autocorrelation tests. The variance ratios are reported in the main rows. The heteroscedasticity-robust test statistics are found in parentheses below the main rows. The random walk null hypothesis implies that the variance ratio is one, and the test statistics have an asymptotic standard normal distribution.[14] Test statistics with an asterisk indicate that their corresponding variance ratios are statistically different from one at the 5% significance level.

---

[13] John Y. Campbell, Andrew W. Lo, and A. Craig MacKinlay, *Econometrics of Financial Markets* (Princeton, N.J. Princeton University Press: 1997): 66-74.

[14] Please refer to chapter 6 for an explanation of the properties of the variance ratio test.

The equal-weighted index-based tests reject the random walk hypothesis for the entire time period and all sub-periods. Furthermore, as in the autocorrelation tests, predictability seems to decrease in the more recent time period and is stronger in the earlier time period. The value-weighted index, on the other hand, shows different patterns. The random walk hypothesis cannot be rejected for any of the time periods or any of the lags, which seems to suggest that those stocks with large market capitalization introduce a relatively higher degree of randomness in their returns behavior - or alternatively expressed – a higher degree of relative market efficiency. This notion of liquidity (or higher market capitalization), which introduces a stronger degree of relative market efficiency is not entirely inconsequential.

As the 1998 September stock market correction and the bailout of Long Term Capital Management (LTCM) showed, one of the underlying premises of asset pricing was flummoxed. When prices move sharply, arbitrage – one of the driving forces of financial economics- does not work with less liquid assets. Hence price movements tend to be unidirectional for the time of perceived or actual lack of liquidity. While the results in table 2.3 could suggest such a phenomenon, the liquidity relationships in pre-emerging markets are more pronounced and therefore give rise to liquidity as one of the most important characteristics in the modeling and valuation of securities.

Table 2.3. Variance ratio empirical results of developed markets

Sample period	Number nq of base observations	Number q of base observations aggregated to form variance ratio			
		2	4	8	16
A. CRSP Equal-weighted index					
62:07:10-94:12:27	1695	1.20 (4.53)*	1.42 (5.30)*	1.65 (5.84)*	1.74 (4.85*
62:07:10-78:10:03	848	1.22 (3.47)*	1.47 (4.44)*	1.74 (4.87)*	1.90 (4.24)*
78:10:10-94:12:27	847	1.19 (2.94)*	1.35 (2.96)*	1.48 (3.00)*	1.54 (2.55)*
B. CRSP Value-weighted index					
62:07:10-94:12:27	1695	1.02 (0.51)	1.02 (0.30)	1.04 (0.41)	1.02 (0.14)
62:07:10-78:10:03	848	1.06 (1.11)	1.08 (0.89)	1.14 (1.05)	1.19 (0.95)
78:10:10-94:12:27	847	0.98 (-0.45)	0.97 (-0.40)	0.93 (-0.50)	0.88 (-0.64)

II.A.3. Autopsy of absolute market efficiency

Overall, those most recent results shed new light upon the efficiency of developed markets as they primarily reject the random walk hypothesis. In this context, a step back into the history of market efficiency research seems appropriate. Most previous research has focused on the statistical approach of testing independence of prices, where most studies have largely accepted the random walk theory of independence.

The history of market efficiency is older than most faculties of finance. In 1964, Paul Cootner published an influential 500-page book titled *The Random Character of Stock Prices*, which contained reprints of all the important work done up to that date. Osborne's theory of Brownian motion and the stock market, Working, Cowles, Alexander, and the full text of Bachelier's 1900 thesis on the theory of speculation can be found.[15] Studies on the subject of stock market efficiency and the first large scale tests of independence were conducted in the period between the early 1960s and the late 1970s. None of the tests have produced evidence of significant non-independence of price changes. This is true for the tests of independence by Cootner, Fama, and Moore.[16] The sample correlation coefficients found were extremely close to zero and thus unanimously supported the independence assumption. Empirical research suggested efficiency.

Nevertheless, over the past few years, some persistent and large irregularities have been detected in developed and sophisticated capital markets. Such irregularities are commonly referred to as market anomalies. Among them are (a) size effects in which firms with low market capitalization seem to produce excess returns, (b) the so-called 'January effect' when stocks seem to produce an excess return during January and (c)

[15] Sidney Alexander, "Price Movements in Speculative Markets: Trends or Random Walks," *Industrial Management Review*, Vol. 2, No. 2 (May 1961):7-26.

Luis Bachelier, *Theory of Speculation* (Paris:Gauthier-Villars, 1900)

Alfred Cowles 3rd, "Can Stock Market Forecaster Forecast?" *Econometrica*, Vol. 1 (July 1933):309-324.

M.F.M. Osborne, "Periodic Structure in the Brownian Movement of Stock Prices," *Operations Research,* Vol. 10, (May-June 1992):245-279.

Holbrook Working, "A Random Difference Series for Use Analysis of Time Series," *Journal of the American Statistical Association*, Vol. 29, (March 1934):11-24.

[16] P.H. Cootner, "Stock Prices: Random vs. Systematic Changes," *Industrial Management Review*, Vol. 3 (Spring 1962):24-45.

E.F. Fama, "The Behavior of Stock Market Prices," *The Journal of Business*, Vol. 38 (Jan. 1965):34-105.

A. Moore, *A Statistical Analysis of Common Stock Prices*, University of Chicago Graduate School of Business Dissertation (1962).

the 'high earnings/price effect', in which stocks trading at high E/P ratios seem to generate excess returns.[17] The debate concerning these market anomalies focuses on the interesting question of whether these are true market inefficiencies or simply results of incorrect measurements of risk or the application of a wrong equilibrium model.

Given the history of market efficiency tests which largely accepted the random walk for developed markets, and the most recent results, which predominantly reject the notion of the random walk, the question must be asked what the value-added of another test of market efficiency is. Different data sets employed, different time intervals, different time periods and the multitude of testing methodologies chosen have not led to any consistent results. Therefore, the measurement of absolute market efficiency may neither mean much to the policy maker nor to the investment manager, since results have not displayed any desired form of consistency.[18] In the context of this book, therefore the only meaning that will be attributed to results from tests of the random walk hypothesis shall be the varying degree of *relative* market efficiency under different time intervals, or relative market efficiency as a comparative measure for securities with different characteristics.

Box 2.0. An intuitive explanation of relative market efficiency

---

A very intuitive explanation of relative market efficiency is demonstrated in the analogy of physical systems suggested by Campbell, MacKinlay and Lo (1997). Physical systems are often evaluated according to their performance in terms of how much energy is used in order to create a specific end-product. For example an engine which uses fuel may only effectively use 80% of the energy to create motion. 20% of the energy contained in the fuel would be lost to heat, light, or noise. Therefore the engine would be 80% energy efficient. The absurdity of engineers trying to use statistical tests to measure whether an engine is efficient or not, delivers the best intuition why only relative efficiency may also be useful for financial markets. The physical laboratory setting of a frictionless world, where absolute efficiency could be measured in an engine, would be as unrealistic as pretending the economic notion of a 'perfect market' applies to securities price behavior.

---

[17] Rolf Haugen, *Modern Investment Theory*, (N.J.: Prentice Hall, 1997),678-92.
This following paper discovers the return differential between value and glamour stocks and it suggests that the differential is a result of expectational errors made by investors, as opposed to a result of a risk-based explanation: Rafael La Porta, Josef Lakonishok, Andrei Shleifer, and Robert Vishny, "Good News for Value Stocks: Further Evidence on Market Efficiency," *Journal of Finance* vol. LII, no. 2 (June 1997): 859-874.
[18] For an interesting article on the real world applicability of strategies based on discovered inefficiencies see: Z. Fluck, B.G. Malkiel, and R.E. Quandt, "The Predictability of Stock Returns: A Cross-Sectional Simulation," *The Review of Economics and Statistics* (March 1996): 176-183.

Accordingly, market efficiency itself will not become an issue of analysis, but rather the dynamic aspect of change in relative market efficiency under different conditions. Measured predictability of securities returns therefore is no judgement against market efficiency but merely a characterization of the returns process in equities, which could indicate a trend of evolving or diminishing relative market efficiency.

II.B. Market efficiency in emerging markets

II.B.1. Overview of methodologies for measuring market efficiency in emerging equity markets

The literature of market efficiency tests concentrating on developing capital markets is less extensive and substantially younger than its predecessor group which solely focused on developed capital markets. The results are more uniform as most studies clearly indicate some form of securities' prices predictability. One reason why the results on market efficiency in emerging markets are less contradictory and more uniform, is due to the fact that most markets have been the subject of only a small number of studies of market efficiency.

Most research focuses on the aggregate index as opposed to individual securities, and does not explore issues pertaining to the causality of changing relative market efficiency. A changing degree of relative market efficiency itself has been discovered in a few studies as various sub-periods have occasionally been individually analyzed. The lack of studies pertaining to the causality of changing market efficiency is also a result of the above mentioned fact that the aggregate index has often been the focus of analysis, as opposed to individual securities. There are exceptions where individual securities were analyzed. Due to the lack of information about individual securities besides market capitalization and industry sector, however, the analyses which were conducted on the securities level did not generate any particularly noteworthy insight.

The case study in this book on the Russian pre-emerging equity market, on the other hand, benefits from a database which contains information on securities characteristics that have not been available to most researchers of market efficiency in emerging equity markets. Particularly, the research coverage proxy index of Russian equities, which has been laboriously obtained from a virtually complete set of global brokerages covering Russian equities, and the details on ADR/GDR programs, are in most cases simply not available to the researcher. Moreover, this case study of the Russian equity market, which is a 'frontier' market or a pre-emerging market, differentiates itself from other studies on emerging market efficiency by the simple fact that the time span analyzed covers the very beginning of the Russian equity market – the genesis period.

The results obtained therefore can be positioned in the larger context of new emerging markets moving onto the radar screen of global investment professionals (see table 2.4.) This establishes a clear difference between this case study and those which have been conducted on mature emerging markets which often act more in line with developed markets and do not display many of the characteristics typical for newly emerging markets.[19]

Table 2.4. Frontier markets

Market	Size Perspective	Dominant Sector	Largest Export Market	Market Cap (US$ bn)
Egypt	Merrill Lynch	Manufacturing	Italy	18.8
Hungary	Cadbury Schweppes	Manufacturing	Germany	8.6
Jordan	Rolls-Royce	Financials	Iraq	5.3
Morocco	Fiat	Financials	France	11.6
Nigeria	Henkel	Manufacturing	US	4.3
Pakistan	BMW	Manufacturing	US	13.7
Poland	Societe Generale	Financials	Germany	11.7
Sri Lanka	Swiss Air	Financials	US	2.6
Venezuela	Barnett Banks	Utilities	US	14.0
Zimbabwe	Silicon Graphics	Financials	South Africa	5.2

Source: IFC, Datastream, Merrill Lynch. Market cap data as of June 30, 1997.

[19] The difference between frontier markets and mature emerging markets, such as Portugal (recently included in MSCI EAFE) or Mexico becomes apparent when looking at the return -volatility profile or the quality of companies in which one can invest.

As table 2.5. demonstrates, there have been a number of studies on market efficiency and descriptive features of emerging equity markets. The following serve as a representative sample of the previous work in the area. Collectively, they demonstrate the most widely used testing methodologies of the random walk assumption and the relative conformity of the obtained results.

Table 2.5.   Studies on market efficiency in emerging markets

Author	Country	Methodology	Results	Date	Time Span	Publication
Hakim	Mexico	Autocorrelation	Weak EMH rejected	1992	1967-1979	Dissertation
Butler And Malaikah	Saudi Arabia, Kuwait	Autocorrelation Non-parametric tests	Kuwait weak EMH not rejected Saudi Arabia weak EMH rejected	1992	1992-1994	Journal of Banking and Finance
Errunza and Losq	Sample of LDC markets	Autocorrelation Runs tests	LDC mkts are less efficient than devpd mkts	1985	1976-1981	Journal of Banking and Finance
Urrutia	Brazil, Argent., Mexico and Chile	Variance Ratio Runs tests	Reject weak EMH for Braz, Arg, Mex, Chile – but under heterosc.-robust test reject only Braz, Chil. and Mex., Runs test does not reject weak EMH for any country	1995	1975-1991	Journal of Financial Research
Ayadi and Pyun	Korea	Variance Ratio	Reject weak EMH under homoscedasticity terms- but not under heteroscedasticity-robust test	1994	1984-1988	Journal of Banking and Finance

Table 2.5. Studies on market efficiency in emerging markets *(continued)*

Author	Country	Methodology	Results	Date	Time Span	Publication
Claessens, Dasgupta, Glen	IFC Emerging Mkts. Database	Autocorrelation Variance Ratio	Partly reject weak EMH	1993	1976/ 1990-1992	World Bank Working Paper
El-Erian and Kumar	Jordan, Turkey, Greece, India, Philippin.	Autocorrelation Runs tests	Largely reject weak EMH	1995	1992-1994	IMF Staff Paper
Rockinger and Urga	Czech Rep., Poland, Hungary and Russia	AR (1) model with time varying parameters	Poland becomes less efficient, Russia becomes more efficient, Czech Republic becomes less efficient initially and more efficient later., Hungary cannot be predicted	1997	1993-1997	Unpublished Working paper
Gordon and Rittenberg	Poland	Test based on intervention in market when price fluctuations exceed +/-10% per day	Reject weak and semi-strong EMH	1995	1993-1994	Comparative Economic Studies

Before describing the individual studies, a short note which shall help to associate the particular methodology with the larger framework of testing for market efficiency, is added at this point.

The virtues and the rationale of the random walk as a tool to test market efficiency will be explained in more detail at a more appropriate place in this book.[20] For now it shall suffice to introduce the random walk in its three forms and their implications for testing methodologies.

Campbell, Lo and MacKinlay define three types of the random walk (RW): RW1 assumes identically and independently distributed increments (IID), RW2 assumes independently and not identically distributed increments (INID), and RW3 assumes uncorrelated increments. RW1 can be

---

[20] See chapter 6. The first section of the chapter explains the linkage between the random walk and the Efficient Market Hypothesis (EMH).

tested with sequences and reversals, and runs tests. RW2 can be tested with filter rules. RW3, the random walk assumption used in this study, can be tested with autocorrelation tests and variance ratio tests.

The notion of the three different random walk assumptions carries a particular weight in the context of pre-emerging markets. There are at least two reasons why the assumption of RW3 in emerging markets appears more optimal than RW1 or RW2: Firstly, RWI assumes IID and RW2 assumes INID. Both assumptions are relatively less representative for pre-emerging markets price behavior where heteroscedasticity and non-normality can be common characteristics. Although RW2 allows for unconditional heteroscedasticity, RW3 remains a safer assumption over RW2 for it does allow some transformation of future price increments to be forecastable using some transformation of past price increments. This RW3 assumption can be defined as:

$$\text{Cov}[\varepsilon_t , \varepsilon_{t-k}] = 0 \text{ for all } k \neq 0 \text{, but where } \text{Cov}[\varepsilon_t^2 , \varepsilon_{t-k}^2] \neq 0 \text{ for some } k \neq 0$$

Accordingly, as opposed to RW1 of RW2, this process has uncorrelated increments but is not independent since its squared increments are correlated in some cases.

Secondly, RW2-based methodologies, such as filter rules or trading rules seem less optimal in the pre-emerging market environment where paper trading simulations (or filter rules based on trading simulations) are difficult, if not impossible, to conduct given the often opaque trading environment where bid/ask quotes may not reflect the real execution price at all times and thus would render a simulation-based test practically meaningless.

As one will see, different authors have used different random walk assumptions and hence different testing methodologies. Interestingly enough, researchers have combined RW1 with RW3 tests many times, which would imply that both the assumption of identically and independently distributed returns and the assumption of uncorrelated increments are used. Often, the exact assumptions were not stated and a parametric test (such as autocorrelation) was complemented by a non-parametric test (such as a runs test). The virtues of runs tests, sequences and reversals tests, the Spearman rank correlation test, or Kendall's τ correlation test, are that non-parametric assumptions can be met. However, often normal asymptotic distributions approximations to the sampling distributions are used, which somewhat defeats the first purpose. Runs tests, as they may not rely on the normal distribution, have severe shortfalls for they do not utilize all the data available.   Runs tests measure signs, not magnitude of change.   Thus valuable information is lost.   For many researchers, the trade-off therefore pointed towards sacrificing statistical orthodoxy by applying parametric or semi-parametric tests to distributions that deviate to a smaller or larger degree from the normal distribution.

When researchers in financial economics had come to realize that the restriction of the identical distribution assumption is quite impractical in financial markets, another set of random walk tests was developed, the random walk 2 (RW2).   RW2 only assumes independent increments, thus it is not making any assumptions about the distribution.   Clearly, under such a test assumption, statistical tests are difficult to conduct.[21]   Nevertheless, filter rules and technical trading rules qualify as tests under RW2.   As one will see in the following review of some of the recent research in the field, Gordon and Rittenberg approach the Polish market with a filter rule.

Finally, there is the random walk 3 (RW3), which enjoys the weakest form of assumptions, namely only uncorrelated increments.   Tests for RW3 have become the most intuitive and most widely used.   The most famous one being the test of autocorrelation, or serial correlation, as some call it. Another test, that has become a superior application to autocorrelation, is the variance ratio test, developed in 1988 by Lo and MacKinlay.[22]

The chapter on new, more insightful tests of market efficiency in the context of the random walk has not been closed yet.   The next step may take the researcher to more dynamic models such as efficiency tests that incorporate Bayesian learning moments and models that more accurately incorporate liquidity conditions in the securities markets and the underlying liquidity constraints in financial services institutions trading in pre-emerging market securities.   For this to be applied to pre-emerging equity markets, more empirical knowledge on the functioning of the equity market and the specific expected utility function of its participants has to be gathered.[23]

---

[21] Due to the understanding that the distribution may not be approximated with any known distribution.

[22] Please refer to chapter 6 for an in-depth discussion of the benefits of the variance ratio test. The variance ratio test has been applied by Ayadi and Pyun (1994); Urrutia (1995); Claessens, Dasgupta and Glen (1993); Campbell, MacKinlay and Lo (1997); Liu and He (1991)

[23] A good introduction of how to apply efficiency tests with Bayesian components in the context of devaluation expectations in the Greek foreign exchange market and the learning component of credibility of policy announcements is given by N. M. Christodoulakis and S.C. Kalyvitis, "Efficiency testing revisited: A foreign exchange market with Bayesian learning," *Journal of International Money and Finance* vol. 16, no. 3 (1997): 367-385.

Besides statistical tests of market efficiency, there have been many alternative schools of thought in pursuit of describing logically why markets may or may not be efficient. As it would be an insurmountable task to review all disciplines in social sciences and natural sciences (such as the theory of Brownian molecular motion which has been applied to markets by Osborne), the most noted have come from the area of behavioral finance.

Behavioral finance has tapped into the rich knowledge of psychiatry and psychology to source new evidence of why markets may not be efficient. This new area of reasoning why markets may not be, and indeed never could be efficient according to conventional definitions, sheds new light on the difference between the macro- and the micro-level of variables explaining the reasons for less efficient markets. Diagram 2.1. demonstrates the two main origins of less efficient markets. The set of variables related to human psychology (or in the cases of the gambler, to psychiatry) can be defined as micro-variables, and the set of variables related to market and institutional infrastructure or information channels can be defined as macro-variables.

Diagram 2.1 Macro and micro variables affecting market efficiency

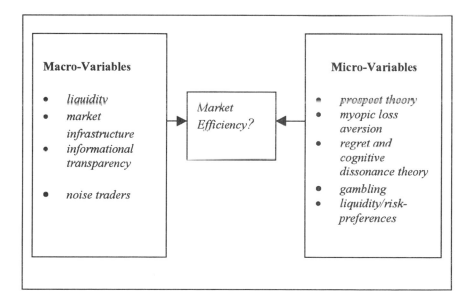

II.B.2. Review of previous studies on market efficiency in emerging equity markets

There are invariably many ways to classify the stages of development in emerging equity markets.[24] Classification schemes could range from market capitalization /GDP to foreign participation in the equity market. Instead of using one fixed measure as a proxy variable for the development stage of an emerging equity market, a number of generally defined measures are used to portray an impressionist image of each developmental stage.

Table 2.6. Evolutionary stages in emerging markets

Stage 1 'hatching'	Stage 2 'pre-emerging'	Stage 3 'emerging'	Stage 4 'mature emerging'
<ul><li>Few quoted companies</li><li>Small mkt capital.</li><li>High sector concentration</li><li>Low liquidity</li><li>High volatility</li><li>Rudimentary institutional setting</li></ul>	<ul><li>Higher liquidity</li><li>Wider variety of companies</li><li>First foreign investors</li><li>Still small mkt cap/GDP</li><li>First equity financing</li><li>Need for institutional market setting is recognized</li></ul>	<ul><li>Less volatile</li><li>Liquidity on the rise</li><li>Securities laws and mkt infrastructure improving rapidly</li><li>First instruments to transfer risk (currency hedging, etc.)</li></ul>	<ul><li>Liquid enough to attract mainstream pension funds in many sectors</li><li>Substantial mkt breadth</li><li>Equity risk prem.-risk-adjusted returns relative to ST money market rates comparable to int'l levels</li></ul>
Romania, Ukraine, Cote d'Ivoire	Russia	Hungary	Mexico, Hong Kong

Despite the large geographical scope of the studies, the research described below has a few features in common. Except for the study by Claessens, Dasgupta and Glen (1993), which encompasses 20 countries that are analyzed over an average time span of ten years, the following individual studies have been selected because the time span examined in the individual

[24] Robert Feldman and Mammohan Kumar, "Emerging Equity Markets: Growth, Benefits, and Policy Concerns," *World Bank Research Observer* (August 1995): 181-200.

studies positions the equity markets analyzed either in stage 1- *'hatching'* or stage 2 – *'pre-emerging'*.

Accordingly, Hakim's exposé of the early Mexican stock market (1967-1979), Ayadi and Pyun's analysis of Korea (1984-1988), Gordon and Rittenberg's assessment of Poland (1993-1994), Urrutia's analysis of sub-periods in Latin and Central American markets (1975-1991), and Errunza and Losq's work on a LDC sample (1976-1981) all belong to either one of the two initial stages during the time span covered in the analysis.

The other studies by Butler and Malaikah on Saudi Arabia and Kuwait (1992-1994), and the study by El-Erian and Kumar on Jordan, India, Turkey, Greece and Philippines (1992-1994) focus on markets that are still in stage 1 or stage 2 of their development.[25] Hence, the markets assessed in the studies described below are in many respects comparable to the Russian equity market development between 1994 and 1997, or for that matter to any pre-emerging or frontier market in the initial genesis period.

While not being immediately relevant and comparable to the situation of the Russian market, the general study on price behavior in emerging stock markets by Claessens, Dasgupta and Glen (1993) presents a fairly comprehensive introduction to the field of analysis of equity returns behavior in emerging markets.[26] In this study, the IFC/World Bank team uses data from the IFC Emerging Markets Database to establish descriptive statistics of security price behavior and to conduct market anomalies and efficiency tests (autocorrelations and variance ratio tests) on twenty emerging markets. Descriptive statistics tests, such as mean, standard deviation, Sharpe ratio, and Jarque-Bera normality tests are complemented by the plotting of mean-variance frontiers. The study of predictability or 'weak-form' efficiency of the individual indices uses autocorrelations, the joint hypothesis Box-Pierce Q-test, and Lo and MacKinlay's (1988) variance ratio test, to control for heteroscedasticity in the data.[27] Furthermore, the authors examine size effects of portfolios on their respective returns by using

---

[25] The cases of Philippines, Turkey and Greece may belong to a more advanced stage than Jordan, India, S. Arabia and Kuwait. However, particularly the closely held Turkish and Greek markets, despite mature foreign interest, are still dominated by features (fixed income/equity-risk-adjusted yield gap) that would point towards stage 2.

[26] S. Claessens, S. Dasgupta and J. Glen, "Stock Price Behavior in Emerging Stock Markets," *World Bank Discussion Series on Emerging Stock Markets* (1996).

[27] A.W. Lo and A MacKinlay, "Stock Market Prices Do Not Follow Random Walks: Evidence from a Simple Specification Test," *The Review of Financial Studies*, Vol.. 1, No. 1 (1988):41-66.

a test which was pioneered by Fama and French (1990).[28] Market anomalies related to seasonality are also tested. This study stands out by the sheer quantity of countries analyzed and the tedious process of creating different portfolios re-sorted by market capitalization for each market in specified time intervals. The authors' conclusion suggests that the markets under scrutiny do not seem to display the most common of the market anomalies found in industrial countries (turn of the year- and small firm-effects). The study does, however, find evidence of predictability of returns (weak-form market inefficiency). Furthermore, normality tests of the returns distribution of individual indices result in the rejection of normality in 18 out of 20 countries at the 1% significance level.

The enormous scope of the study did not allow for an in-depth venture into emerging market-specific factors possibly responsible for anomalies, such as liquidity-enhancing structures in place, or transparency-enhancing structures, such as research coverage or Western auditors. Moreover, it does not touch upon explanatory variables possibly nurturing a higher degree of market efficiency over time, such as declining political risk or liquidity and transparency facilitators. Lastly, the date of the study (1993) did not allow the inclusion of any of the East European markets, and for that matter, the Russian equity market or other pre-emerging markets of the most recent time periods.

Building on a previous study on the Mexican stock market conducted by Ortiz (1980), who performed a runs test based on monthly prices for 79 shares for the 1967-1979 period, Hakim's (1992) study on the efficiency of the Mexican stock market applies a serial correlation test on returns.[29] The early time period examined in the Mexican market offers interesting parallels to the Russian frontier market, especially with regard to foreign investor participation and shareholder rights protection. Mexico, during that time was also comparable to Russia as it neighbors the US and thus was of immense interest to foreign investors throughout its entire market development cycle.

Russia, given its political legacy and its proximity to the West European investment centers, as well, was on the investor radar screen virtually from day one. Thus, it belongs in the general category of 'pull' markets, which

---

[28] E. Fama, "Efficient Capital Markets II," *Journal of Finance* (1991):1575-1617.
[29] Miguel Hakim, "The Efficiency of the Mexican Stock Market" (Ph.D. diss., Claremont University, 1988)

attract foreign interest regardless.[30] 'Push' markets, such as Jordan, Kuwait, Saudi Arabia, on the other hand, are characterized by the fact that the burden of attracting foreign investment is solely on them. In other words, international investors can easily live without them, and index weights will be small or zero.

Hakim's study examines the correlation coefficient between past returns and future returns $p(Ri_t, Ri_{t-1})$. An estimate of p will tell if the return series follows a random walk. As the random walk model states that any price change is independent of the sequence of the previous price changes, it would imply that the autocorrelations of the returns on any security are zero for all lags. Hakim shows sample autocorrelations using weekly returns for 91 stocks. The time periods vary from stock to stock but on average run from 1972 to 1981. Under the hypothesis that the true autocorrelation is zero, the sample autocorrelations for lags greater than zero are normally distributed with mean zero and standard deviation 1/square root of the number of observations. In the weekly return analysis with lag one, Hakim discovers that 28 of the autocorrelations are statistically different form zero. Of the 28, 23 are negative. This indicates that the market overreacts. Additionally, Hakim investigates the stationarity over time of the negative serial correlation for Mexican securities by dividing the 1972-1981 period into five-year sub-periods. The results show that statistical significance of the negative autocorrelations was quite consistent over time. Thereby this study touched upon the issue of autocorrelation being a function of the inherent non-stationarity of the data. By examining the individual sub-periods and by finding consistency with the overall period, it is assumed that a possible non-stationarity effect will not have been solely responsible for autocorrelation.

Another study by Butler and Malaikah (1992) examines the stock markets of Saudi Arabia and Kuwait.[31] This study appears to be relevant in a pre-emerging market context primarily in the sense that both Russia and Saudi Arabia initially suffered from severe liquidity constraints as a consequence of a poorly organized trading infrastructure.[32] Applying autocorrelations and non-parametric runs tests, the authors find that Kuwaiti stocks have mean lag one 0.053 autocorrelation. Of all stocks analyzed in Kuwait, 36% have statistically significant autocorrelations and 72% of these

---

[30] The terminology of 'push' and 'pull' markets is derived from the on-line industry, where web sites which disseminate ("push") their products to one's terminal without the user having to actively download, or 'pull' the information from the server.

[31] K.C. Butler and S.J. Malaikah, "Efficiency and Inefficiency in Thinly Traded Stock Markets," *Journal of Banking and Finance*, vol. 16, iss. 1 (February 1992): 197-210.

[32] Prior to the introduction of the Russian Trading System (RTS) in Fall 1995.

are positively autocorrelated (of which 43% are statistically significant at the 5% level). This finding is in line with those results found in studies on developed markets. Fama reports that 37% of all stocks have statistically significant autocorrelations in developed markets.

The results found for Saudi Arabia are quite different. In Saudi Arabia, all 35 stocks examined have negative and statistically significant autocorrelations. The mean autocorrelation is -0.471. The magnitude of autocorrelation is also much larger than in other markets. A study done by Conard and Jutter (1973) found that unusually high autocorrelations in the German market resulted in the mean absolute lag one autocorrelation of 0.271. As another comparison, Fama reports that for a relatively efficient market (30 large stocks of the NYSE) the mean absolute lag one autocorrelation was 0.048.

Butler and Malaikah's (1992) study differentiates itself from previous works by adding the runs test which does not require the assumption of normally distributed returns. This test fully supported the previous autocorrelation results. This study concluded that Saudi Arabia, where banks have a brokerage monopoly but are prohibited from owning stock, and where specialists and official market makers do not exist to promote liquidity, the statistically significant autocorrelations found would possibly not translate into a trading rule that consistently generates excess profits due to the doubtfulness of whether trades could actually be executed at the prices quoted in the data. Butler and Malaikah, therefore proved the existence of market inefficiency in Saudi Arabia. The authors hint at illiquidity resulting from the particular trading infrastructure as a possible explanation.

A study conducted by Errunza and Losq (1985) sheds light upon the behavior of security prices for a sample of LDC markets, in which, with the exception of a few Mexican firms, no significant foreign portfolio investments existed in the sample countries in 1985.[33] Therefore, results and testing frameworks could be compared to the pre-emerging markets of Central Asia - many of them still characterized by severe capital inflow controls - that are in similar positions to the countries in the sample: Argentina, Brazil, Chile, Greece, Jordan, Korea, Mexico, Thailand, Zimbabwe and India (all in 1985).

The first part of the study examines the above mentioned markets for empirical distributions of log price changes by testing for normality of

---

[33] V.R. Errunza and E. Losq, "The Behavior of Stock Prices on LDC Markets," *Journal of Banking and Finance*, Vol. 16, (1985):561-575.

distribution and non-stationarity of variance. The second part tests for independence of price changes by applying autocorrelation analysis and runs tests. The study finds that the examined LDC markets display probability distributions consistent with log normal distributions and in some cases exhibit non-stationary variance. Through estimated serial correlation coefficients and corroborated by runs tests, the study also shows that LDC markets are less efficient than more developed capital markets. The authors speculate that the lesser degree of market efficiency observed in LDC markets results from barriers to the dissemination of information, such as loose financial disclosure requirements, slowing down the speed of information dissemination.

The study on the Korean market covering the time span from 1984 to 1988 by Ayadi and Pyun (1994) becomes relevant in the Russian pre-emerging market context as it contrasts the fact that the Russian market was open to foreign investors during the time span analyzed in this study, whereas until 1991 foreigners were only allowed to invest in Korean securities indirectly through special investment trusts. The methodology used is the variance ratio test, pioneered by Lo and MacKinlay (1988), in order to investigate the behavior of prices of stocks traded on the Korean securities exchange within the general framework of the random walk hypothesis.[34] The virtue of the variance ratio test is its capability to apply a test-statistic under both homoscedastic and heteroscedastic error terms. Following this test, the authors reject the random walk under the homoscedasticity assumption, but cannot reject the random walk under the heteroscedasticity-robust assumption. While this paper applies a possibly superior model of measuring market efficiency it falls short of exploring causal relationships of market efficiency. The authors briefly note government intervention as being the reason for price predictability but refrain from further analysis of other factors possibly promoting a higher degree of efficiency.

Urrutia (1995) examines Latin American equity markets with respect to market efficiency.[35] As will be demonstrated for the case of Russia, Urrutia also finds that Brazil, Argentina, Chile and Mexico do not follow a normal distribution. Furthermore, Urrutia also refers to the phenomenon of noise trading as a possible cause of the rejection of the random walk. In this study,

---

[34] O.F. Ayadi and C.S. Pyun, "An Application of Variance RatioTests to the Korean Securities Market," *Journal of Banking and Finance*, Vol. 18, Issue 4, (September 1994):643-658.

[35] J.L. Urrutia, "Tests of Random Walk and Market Efficiency for Latin American Equity Markets," *Journal of Financial Research*, Vol. 18, Issue 3, (Fall 1995):299-309.

Urrutia uses the variance ratio test and a runs test. Using monthly data of equity indices of Brazil, Argentina, Chile and Mexico for the period between 1975-1991, the variance ratio test rejects the random walk hypothesis for Brazil, Argentina, Chile and Mexico. The heteroscedasticity-robust variance ratio test confirms the findings for all countries except for Argentina. A runs test is also conducted and finds that prices follow the random walk.

Gordon and Rittenberg's (1995) study on the efficiency of the Polish equity market clearly differentiates itself from other works as it deals with a pre-emerging market and the non-accessibility of reliable data which would lend itself to econometric analysis.[36] Gordon and Rittenberg solve the problem by conducting a qualitative assessment of the fulfillment of the five assumptions underlying market efficiency (see above for the listing of the five assumptions). The methods used may not neatly fit into the conventional literature of market efficiency in emerging markets, however, the elements of behavioral finance discussed are clearly relevant for a pre-emerging market such as Russia, where the lack of hard facts must often be substituted by soft-reasoning and actions derived thereof.[37]

Using public survey data and press releases, Gordon and Rittenberg find that the first assumption of investors acting rationally is violated. The main proof is derived from statements that indicate a strong reliance on the perception that great performance in the past can be projected into the future, and that the 'fashion' of stocks dictates their future performance. This notion is closely connected to a phenomenon that has become known among psychologists as "anchoring."[38] Subsequently, assumptions 2-5 are scrutinized in light of the circumstances prevailing at the Warsaw Stock Exchange. The authors find that assumption 2, which premises price taking behavior, is violated by the non-existence of an insider trading law. Moreover, the large demand for new brokerage accounts revealed the unpreparedness of brokers to absorb large volumes and led to time deficiencies when placing orders or setting up accounts. This violated assumption 5, which requires investors to react quickly and accurately to new information. The same assumption was also violated by the imposition of a 10% daily limit on share price movements. Due to this limit, in many

---

[36] B. Gordon and L. Rittenberg, "The Warsaw Stock Exchange: A test of market efficiency," *Comparative Economic Studies*, vol. 39, no. 2 (Summer 1995).

[37] Soft-reasoning prevails when numbers and facts are only scarcely available. As investors still need to make decisions in many such situations, soft-reasoning sometimes bordering on charlatanism is used to form an opinion on market sentiment.

[38] Robert Shiller, "Human Behavior and the Efficiency of the Financial System," (www.econ.yale.edu/~shilller/handbook.html), 43.

cases 'new information' could neither 'quickly' nor 'accurately' be reflected in the share price.

The authors of this study have abstained from any conventional tests of market efficiency but instead have designed a test based on the 10% band limit of daily share price movements. Logic dictates that on any day when returns reach the +/-9.5% target, an intervention would take place. This would imply that shares do not fully adjust to the new information available and thus the semi-strong form EMH would be rejected. In 39% of all trading days such intervention takes place. It follows that a carryover effect would take place the following day. This hypothesis is also proven valid. Furthermore, a trading strategy is devised that exploits the carryover effect which is 'knowledgeable' information on the day the intervention by the specialist takes place. With this trading strategy, which outperforms a simple buy-and-hold strategy, the weak-form EMH is also rejected.[39]

Another interesting study has been conducted by El-Erian and Kumar (1995).[40] It broadly discusses comparative features of equity markets in Jordan, Turkey, Greece, India and the Philippines before venturing into such subjects as informational efficiency and determinants of stock market development. While the development stage of particularly Jordan and India, both strong representatives of 'push' markets, are comparable to the first period in the Russian equity market, India seems to impose many more obstacles to foreign investors than Russia ever has.

Two tests are conducted on the market efficiency of the respective equity markets. Firstly, an autocorrelation test is conducted, which rejects the random walk for Jordan, Turkey and the Philippines. Secondly, a runs test is conducted, as the authors express concern that serial coefficients may be dominated by a few unusual and extreme price changes which possibly could obscure a tendency toward a coherent pattern of price changes. The runs test does not depend on the finite variance assumption of the price changes.

The results for the non-parametric runs test confirm that all countries exhibit significant positive serial correlation, except for India. Lastly, the authors discuss means of improving equity markets in Middle Eastern countries. In this study, an aggregate index was used which, due to the averaging effect of index creation, would most likely exhibit more

---

[39] See also Christopher Bobinski, "Warsaw Begins to Recover," *Financial Times*, 22 April 1994, 37.

[40] Mohamed A. El-Erian and Mammohan S. Kumar, "Emerging Equity Markets in Middle Eastern Countries," *IMF Staff Papers*, vol, 32, no.2 (1995): 313-344.

systematic patterns, than those which would be observed on an individual security level. Again, this study delivers a snapshot result of dependence of securities returns. It does not explore changing patterns over time, or causal effects of serial dependence besides some qualitative speculation in inefficiency of information dissemination.

II.B.3. Behavioral finance offers clues to the reasons of market inefficiency

In the context of market efficiency in frontier emerging markets, Shiller's (1997) critique of rational investor behavior adds a valuable viewpoint to the current literature.[41] Particularly in frontier emerging markets, where informational shortage and barriers often prevail, investors have to strongly rely on factors such as market sentiment. Market sentiment, traditionally a soft and only imprecisely defined factor, can then become a function of processes that are best described with theories of behavioral finance.

Shiller points out that investors are frequently acting irrationally as demonstrated by prospect theory, myopic loss aversion, or regret and cognitive dissonance theory. Particularly, the theory of regret and cognitive dissonance delivers potential answers to the question of why emerging markets analysts tend to consciously overlook the data which would lead them to believe that stock prices are no longer justified as long as favorable brokerage reports are produced, even in the absence of supportive fundamental data. This theory also highlights the importance of authority that is associated with research reports, and their impact on investors. In other words, as long as research reports support past investment decisions the possible failure in the performance of the stock will not be recognized and regret about a false decision will not be realized, and postponed as long as possible. This sequence of actions is uniquely dangerous in the context of frontier emerging markets. While in developed markets reality will reassert itself sooner rather than later (for example through quarterly earnings reports), in frontier emerging markets – an environment best described by data scarcity – reality can take years to reassert itself. In the meantime, decisions are made by humans, who are always susceptible to the shortcomings explained by behavioral finance.

The theory of the disjunction effect which states that there is a tendency for people to want to wait to make decisions until some type of information

---

[41] Robert Shiller, "Human Behavior and the Efficiency of the Financial System," (www.econ.yale.edu/~shilller/handbook.html).

is released, even if the information is not really important for the decision, reveals a very remarkable phenomenon in pre-emerging market investing. A representative example of the disjunction effect was given during the frantic market nervousness surrounding Yeltsin's heart surgery in fall 1996.

The Russian equity market traded on faxes which depicted a diagram of Yeltsin's heart and every investor made her own assessment of whether or not the president of Russia would have a successful operation. Even if Yeltsin had died during this operation, the former Communists could have done nothing to interrupt the process of building a free market economy, as they lacked both broad support and legislative or executive force to reverse Russia's transition into a free society. The realistic improbability of a re-nationalization and expropriation of industry, did not matter to the 'irrationally' acting analyst, who for disjunction effect-based reasons, needed this extra bit of information to allocate additional assets to the Russian equity market.

Finally, the theory of gambling and speculation, which statistically supports the existence of between 1% and 3% of the population who are pathological gamblers (as such recognized by the American Psychiatric Association), also contributes an element of irrational behavior and therefore behavior which does not conform with the assumptions underlying the EMH.[42] The assumption that the percentage of pathological gamblers in pre-emerging market professions is probably even larger than in the general population, would further support the view that EMH in emerging markets is under threat by market participants who have come to realize that frontier emerging market investing often replicates a casino atmosphere. In such an environment, market behavior could be explained by utility functions that become concave upward in extremely high range, and thus lead to irrational behavior not in line with the assumptions of the EMH.

Behavioral finance has opened the debate for new explanations of why markets may not be efficient. Fuller and Thaler, two academics-turned fund managers have taken the ideas a step further and launched a mutual fund based on models trying to exploit identified market inefficiencies. A few examples which underpin such models are given on the website (www.fullerthaler.com):

---

[42] D.W. Bolen and W.H. Boyd, "Gambling and the Gambler: A Review and Preliminary Findings," *Archives of General Psychiatry,* 18, 5 (1968): 617-629.

1. **Behavioral Finance/Economics Non-Economic Behavior**

    - Agency Problems: Compensation of analysts and portfolio managers causes them to not act in their client's best interests. Example: 'window dressing' at the end of a fiscal quarter. In such a situation fund managers sell or buy securities which have underperformed or outperformed, respectively, in order to reveal them, or not, in the quarterly publicly available holdings report. This is particularly true in frontier emerging markets. After the meltdown of the Russian equity market and the ricochet effect leading to defaults and quasi-liquidations of hedge funds (Long Term Capital Management) and resignations of CEOs (UBS, etc.), many portfolio managers took the risk of missing a rally in emerging markets, rather than 'making the same mistake twice' and as a consequence losing their jobs. The other effect was that many portfolio managers shunned risk altogether and consequently missed many opportunities for their shareholders. The agency problem is probably the single most dangerous interference with rational market behavior. Most portfolio managers are evaluated in short-term intervals and as a consequence investment theses that would expose the portfolio to the risk of a waiting period cannot be taken. Naturally, this implies that institutional investors mostly follow rallies rather than capture the entire upside (a good example would be deep cyclical stocks.)

    - Regret (Prospect Theory): The pain of losses exceeds the pleasure of gains or "The disposition to hold losers too long and sell winners too soon." (Shefrin and Statman, Journal of Finance, 1985). The failure of sell-discipline is most pronounced in institutional asset management departments where portfolio action is often only initiated when stock prices turn and previously gained profits evaporate, not when fair valuation of an equity has been reached, or when stocks slip below their cost base.

    - Lack of Self Control: "Dollar Cost Averaging." (Statman, Journal of Portfolio Management, 1995)

2. **Behavioral Finance/Economics Some Heuristic Biases:** Typically the cause of cognitive errors

    - Anchoring: Forecasters tend to under/over-react to new information.

- Saliency, Recency: Humans tend to over-estimate the probability of a future currency crisis if they have recently heard about a currency crisis (a phenomenon that is closely linked to the theory of memes – see chapter 10).

- Extrapolation: Recency and saliency tend to cause forecasters to naively extrapolate and overreact to new information during times of crisis or shortly thereafter.

- Overconfidence: Human beings tend to be overly confident about how much they know. This is particularly true in a profession such as active asset management, which is fighting an intensifying battle against passively managed indexed funds. Any weakness in market knowledge would make the position of the active fund manager even more vulnerable than it already has become. Hence, overconfidence is a protective mechanism that is not always based on sound knowledge.

- Framing: When solving problems, we tend to frame or analyze the problem in well defined ways, based upon our education, training, and experience. Sometimes, we cannot break out of the framework when we should. A good example is the traditional fundamental investors' bias against internet stocks, which require an new valuation framework in order to justify the early 1999 valuations. In an emerging market context, framing surfaced as a problem when economists initially applied currency crisis models of the 1970s and 1980s to the Asian crisis, only to realize later that their applicability and utility is no longer useful in the Asian context where new models were required.

Chapter 3

Frontier Emerging Equity Market Infrastructure
The valuation dimension of equity infrastructure

The notion that topics related to the infrastructure of an equity market are best delegated to the global custodian or the compliance department associated with an asset manager could not be more ill-perceived in pre-emerging markets. Both, the emerging market portfolio manager and the policy maker on the ground, should find ample utility in understanding the progress of equity market infrastructure developments. The extent of development in the equity market infrastructure translates directly into the degree of informational and operational efficiency. The hallmark of operational efficiency are smooth trading, clearing, settlement, and custody systems.

One of the prerequisites of informational efficiency is a set of transparent and unambiguously interpretable legal and regulatory, tax, and accounting disclosure rules. This chapter will use the example of the Russian equity market to demonstrate the progress and the remaining problems in the areas of clearing, settlement, trading, custody, legal and regulatory, tax, and accounting rules, and how a lack of progress can severely impact the valuation dimension of the equity market.

The second purpose of this chapter is to familiarize the reader with the essentials of the frontier equity environment and the continuous progress that has been taking place in alleviating the investment obstacles that have existed, and to some degree still do. Again, the case of Russia will serve as a case study to illustrate major obstacles and progress. For practical purposes, this chapter also gives the reader a reference framework for developments in the equity market infrastructure of Russia. The most reliable, current, and accessible source of information about changes in the Russian equity market infrastructure, are a number of web sites sponsored by official Russian bodies and domestic and international brokerages. Thus, where applicable, reference to appropriate web sites will be made. The rise of internet technology has changed the barriers of entry in frontier market investing. While on-line, web-enabled information is often general in nature and therefore possesses questionable utility when reliable and concise information is required in order to make investment decisions, the sheer availability facilitates a much wider participation in newly emerging equity markets. Substantially lower barriers of entry in the field of asset management, primarily due to free information, will become a factor with which venerable professional asset managers have yet to fully come to grips. This factor will also be responsible for an accelerated investment process and a more volatile frontier equity environment.[1]

This chapter will begin by outlining the story of the genesis and emergence of the Russian equity market. Subsequently, the topics of clearing, settlement, trading, custody, legal and regulatory, tax, and accounting rules will be addressed. Finally, a snapshot overview will be given on Russian equity market infrastructure, outlining the reasons for the existing valuation gap between Russia and other emerging markets.

III.A.   The early equity market

III.A.1.   Genesis of the Russian equity market

The Russian voucher privatization formally ended June 30, 1994.[2] By that time a total number of 13,832 enterprises had been sold and 97% of the

---

[1] A good example of free information and low trading fees is the US internet equity sector. This sector is primarily driven by day traders who use low-transaction fee on-line brokerages for purchases and sales of securities, and the vast information resources of the internet to learn about their investments in the internet sector. As a consequence of the rise of these more or less professional, and rather less fundamental value-oriented investors, the internet sector has become the most volatile and most 'shocking' experience in equity investing during 1998 and 1999. It is now simply a matter of time until frontier markets will be tradable for below $10 per transaction via on-line brokerages. The implication will be enormous. Most importantly, liquidity will be dramatically enhanced and investor sophistication dramatically reduced.

[2] For a detailed description of the process of Russia's stabilization process, the political and economic forces underlying the privatization process please refer to: Anders Aslund, *How Russia Became a Market Economy* (Washington, D.C.: The Brookings Institution, 1995)

population enjoyed direct or indirect ownership in companies. The simplified process by which foreigners obtained shares in the Russian companies can be described as follows and is also quite representative for other newly emerging equity markets in the region, such as Ukraine and Romania.

The initial owners of shares, or certificates that serve as share proxies, were employees, private citizens and the Federal Property Fund.[3] Quickly, a new profession emerged: the regional broker. This first type of intermediary between buyers and sellers of shares (or vouchers in some cases) has a keen sense of making money by shrewdly assessing the demand for equities of specific companies. The regional broker, often associated with the share registries or the companies themselves, prefers to create quasi-monopolies in the sourcing of specific stock, which are conceptually not too different from the role of the market-maker on the RTS (Russian Trading System) which was created in late 1995. It is not unusual that the regional broker is an insider in the company.

The next intermediary is the Moscow broker, who sources shares from the regional broker, of course, often at an arbitrary premium. The Moscow broker benefits by feeding the shares largely into the international market. The first points of contact are the Moscow-based offices of the international brokerage companies. Other international brokers also become involved at this point. Again, everyone pays a sizeable premium to the Moscow broker. Later in the Russian development, and particularly in Ukraine and Romania, it had become desirable for the international brokers to set up their own voucher and stock scouting teams to comb the countryside and knock on the doors of relatively unsophisticated local shareholders in order to decrease the accumulated premia by disintermediating the army of regional and national brokers.[4] The VTsIOM poll conducted in December 1993 shows the

---

[3] Once vouchers were collected, they could be used to bid for shares in companies during voucher auctions. Anyone was entitled to participate in such auctions, local citizens, voucher funds, and also foreigners. As a result of Chubais' efforts, the rules of voucher distribution and voucher auctions were quite liberal and essentially based on free markets. In reality, however, voucher auctions were often closed affairs among local constituents, employers, and the occasional voucher fund. Although 35% of shares were to be exchanged for vouchers, in reality only an average of 20% were exchanged for vouchers. The rest were sold for cash or kept in some form of employee accounts. As a result, most shares had gone to local or company insiders and many of Russia's most valuable companies managed to evade voucher privatization completely. (see S. Mikhoilov, Once Again About the Results and Problems of Privatization in 1993," *Ekonomicheskaya gazeta*, no. 19, May 1993.

[4] The creation of international "voucher vulture" teams began mainly in 1994, with a second wave during 1996/7. In the earlier time period, Russian voucher vultures exclusively

following results of what Russians had done with their voucher certificates: 26% chose to buy shares in a voucher fund, 25% sold their vouchers, and 7% gave them away. Fifteen percent bought shares in an enterprise close to their own work or a family member's employment, 8% bought shares in other enterprises unrelated to their own employment or that of family or friends. Twenty-five percent were undecided about what to do with their vouchers.[5] These numbers are indicative of most pre-emerging market shareholder bases generated through voucher privatization. First and foremost, voucher investments were based on stakeholder interests not on shareholder interests.

The typical pre-emerging market voucher investor is more concerned about maintaining employment than about equity returns in recently privatized companies. This, obviously, does not nurture a shareholder-oriented, but rather a stakeholder-oriented, equity culture. Accordingly, 'voucher vulture' teams are instrumental in generating sizeable share and voucher blocks to reach a critical mass for foreign institutional equity participation.

At the point of early share or voucher transfer between retail sellers and professional buyers, prices were set more or less arbitrarily since no central pricing mechanism was in place. Valuation rules were quite undeveloped and the initial seller received a price that was somewhat inversely correlated to the remoteness of the transaction from Moscow, where anyone involved in capital markets had a better idea of how to gauge the demand for specific equities, than relatively unsophisticated sellers in the provinces. Gradually, some basic valuation rules came into fashion. Due to the absence of any financial information, the most common valuation practice was to estimate how many cents to pay for a barrel of reserves or ton of capacity (oil and metal companies), or how many cents to pay for reported tonnage (shipping companies). Natural resource stocks, everyone understood, could be assessed with the proxy of global commodity prices. The extractability of

---

targeted vouchers, mainly from the relatively uneducated rural population During 1996/97 voucher vultures primarily began targeting actual share certificates in second- and third-tier companies. The phenomenon of voucher vultures has become a contemptuous issue in pre-emerging markets, often reducing the popular acceptance of initially well-received privatization programs. On the other hand, voucher vultures have been instrumental in providing the necessary liquidity for the equity market by channeling vouchers and shares into the superregional trading centers and finally into the international markets. Without this mechanism of changing ownership from unmotivated shareholders to active shareholders, management lethargy and share illiquidity would be far greater problems than we actually can observe today.

[5] Yelena Dzhaginova, "A Quarter of the Population in Russia Do Not Know What to Do With Their Vouchers," *Segodnya*, January 26, 1994.

the resources or the quality of management remained highly subjective parameters.

Only gradually, and only for those companies whose management was open and responsive to questions, could Western brokerage firms start writing their first research reports. In those research reports numbers were still not the centerpiece of information, but rather individual companies' operations were qualitatively assessed with occasional sales estimates, and an opinion on their general survivability. If management was forthcoming, the assessment of management and strategy generally was positive. Nevertheless, despite the information vacuum, no less than $600 million of foreign portfolio investment was estimated to have found its way into the Russian equity market by September 1994.[6]

Most buyers were dedicated emerging markets funds with a fairly high degree of sophistication. Others were 'instividuals' (an individual with institutional purchasing power). All of them were presumably in this market because it was the "greatest asset sale the world had seen."

III.A.2. Emergence of an equity market

The initial euphoria of the Russian equity market was not sustainable. While the AKM Industrial Index had risen from 1 to 25 between October 1993 and September 1994, it retreated by 40% in the following twelve months. Liquidity was very low and the trading action of a few institutional buyers had disproportionate effects on stock prices. This early Russian experience was truly the pioneering work of a few dedicated investors. Investments were made in the absence of fundamental research and stock prices were solely liquidity driven. Stock prices were liquidity driven for the whole of 1996, but at least starting after the elections in July 1996, liquidity and flow of funds into stocks became a function of not only supply but also some fundamental criteria, which became available and were deemed to be relevant for the assessment of equities.

---

[6] Salomon Brothers, *Russian Equities Road Map-A Bullish View of the Bear*, (September 1995). This number varies, other brokers, such as Flemings estimates total foreign holdings at $2.5 bn by mid-1995.

This number has to be compared to a total market capitalization of about $20bn by end-1995. (Fleming Research, *Russia Coming in from the Cold*, August 1996.)

The concept of supply creating demand ceased to be valid in the second part of 1996. It was rather the brokerage community that became the 'king makers' of selected stocks. Those stocks were to become the first Russian blue-chips, and not surprisingly they did not differ very much from the 'blue chips' that were bought during the initial euphoria phase. Blue chip material was thought to be found in oil, gas, utility, telecommunications companies, and in the occasional shipping and paper company.

Chart 3.0. AKM Industrial Index (Sep 1993 – Jan 1998)

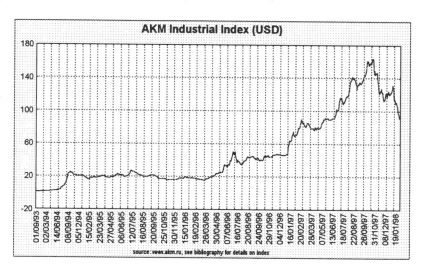

III.B. Equity market infrastructure

III.B.1. Regulatory system

The legal environment for the Russian equity market just recently has become less opaque to the foreign investor. Since the first dedicated law on the Russian securities market appeared on December 28, 1991, the three main agencies: Central Bank of Russia (CBR), Ministry of Finance (Minfin), and the Securities and Exchange Commission (SEC), have been trying to organize the market in the most efficient way. This process has frequently revealed the underlying politics of the interest groups rather than a focus on the most efficient way to regulate the market. The current structure of securities market regulation can be viewed in diagram 3.0.

Diagram 3.0. Regulatory structure in the Russian frontier market

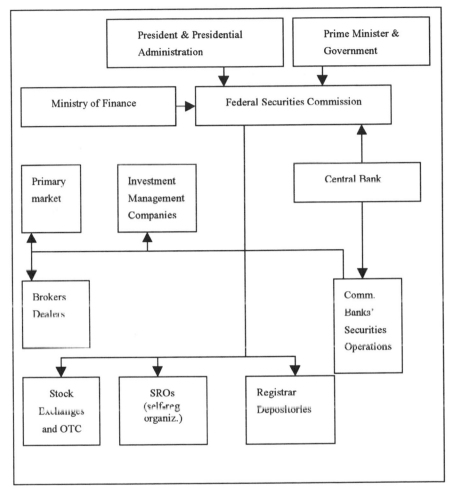

Source: Nomura Securities, 1997

The main regulations affecting Russian equity offerings and trading are summarized in table 3.0. and found on the website of the Federal Commission for the Russian Securities Market (FCSM),

http://www.fe.msk.ru/lat/win/infomarket/fedcom/ewhatsnew.html,

which is the most reliable and most current source of changes affecting the regulatory environment of the Russian equity market. This website also contains an archive of all the historical statutes and amendments. Due to the continuously changing nature of the regulatory environment, the following descriptions in table 3.0. shall merely serve as a snapshot true as of early 1998, and the interested reader should consult the live-updates on the website of the Federal Securities and Exchange Commission.

Table 3.0. *Key laws and regulations*

Key Laws and Regulations	
Regulation	Main focus
Law on the Securities Market (April 1996)	Regulates professional market participants Established procedures for share issues Established structure and responsibilities of the FCSM
Law on Joint Stock Companies (Jan 1996)	Regulates corporate governance, shareholder meeting rules, and information disclosure rules by companies
Presidential Decree " On Measures to Improve the Investment Policy of the Russian Federation (Jul 1995)	Establishes mutual funds
FCSM Regulations nos. 3,6, and 18 (Jul 1195-Sept 1996)	Regulates shareholder registries
FCSM Regulation No. 20 (Oct. 1996)	Regulates custodians
FCSM Regulation No. 22 (Dec. 1996)	Regulates broker dealers

Source: Brunswick Brokerage, Federal Commission of the Securities Markets

One of the main issues for all pre-emerging markets is the enforceability of the regulatory framework. In Russia's case - although the Law on Joint Stock companies which came into effect January 1, 1997 criminalizes securities fraud - the 'teeth' of the enforcing agency, the FCSM, have not been seen. Much of the enforceability is a matter of having sufficient resources to oversee the entire market, which due to its decentralized location and the frequent absence of superregional co-ordination, can cause problems. However, only recently the Russian FCSM has expanded its staff from 100 to almost 300 officers, and has initiated the process of actively investigating complaints. Most of the issues that have been covered by the media have dealt with conflicts between minority and majority shareholders. Updates on regulatory issues can also be obtained from: http://www.skate.ru., or via The Skate Report-Capital Markets Russia, which is produced in association with the Moscow Times.

III.B.2. Clearing and settlement

In the case of Russia, there is no central clearinghouse or central depository. Trades are settled on a trade-by-trade basis through simple re-registration. The registry system in Russia is decentralized. Every company with more than 500 shareholders must declare an independent registry. The FCSM is in charge of licensing new registries. Licensed registries are required to have at least 25 issuers' registries with more than 500 shareholders each, or at least 10,000 shareholder accounts. The idea behind this regulation is to stimulate consolidation in the industry. As can be seen in table 3.1., some progress has already been achieved with some of the Moscow-based registries attracting several of the large issuers' registries. Previously, the standard for each issuer was to create an independent subsidiary, which then became the legally required 'independent' registry. Via this set-up, the registry remained quasi-in-house and the risk of shareholder exclusion, wrongful deletion from the books, or refusal to enter into transactions always remained an option for the company. Arbitrary deletion from the registry has not happened for some time in Russia.

The story of a major shareholder locked out of the factory by the security guard, however, still is a last resort of conversation at cocktail parties among wealthy, older, and less astute Russia investors who dearly enjoy portraying themselves as the 'Indiana Jones' fighting a Soviet-type environment. As long as those stories circulate, and the risk of actual deletion from the company registry is perceived as real, a generous discount to other emerging markets will prevail in Russian valuations, as well as in other pre-emerging markets which provide such evidence for stories turning into journalistic gossip, and ultimately affecting the risk premium in an often disproportionate manner.

The effects of anecdotal evidence of shareholder mistreatment cannot be underestimated. Emerging market brokers in New York and London are infamous for taking a quick and sometimes negatively biased view of the less shareholder-friendly markets in Eastern Europe and Africa. Any shareholder-unfriendly action becomes an integral part of the conversational archive of market participants in emerging markets. This archive is opened at any possible occasion when 'war stories' are on the conversational agenda – which is the case at most emerging markets conferences where some market participants gather to assess each other's hierarchy of emerging market experience.

Some markets are learning their lessons well and quickly. For example, in December of 1998, when one of Poland's largest listed companies misled investors by inadequately informing them about contractual obligations related to the degree of ownership of a cellular operator. An undisclosed contract required the sale of a substantial part of the stake to a third party at a fraction of the estimated market price, which would clearly destroy shareholder value. In this case, the government reacted swiftly by imposing a considerable monetary penalty and by requiring management changes. Poland's image as a transparent market, while harmed in the first place, was preserved as much as was possible. A market de-rating or a rising risk premium did not follow the initial event. Overall, it was a well-managed market infrastructure crisis that otherwise could have taken on a life of its own, and caused substantially more damage.[7]

Table 3.1. Large Shareholder Registries

Registry	Issuer
Center-Invest	Chernogorneft, Sidanka, Varyeganneftegaz, Kondpetroleum
Inkol	Rostelekom, Saratovsteklo, Smolensk Sviazinfrom
Irkutskoe Fondovoe Agentstvo	Irkutskenergo, Irkutsk Eletrosviaz, Baikal Pulp and Paper
Moscow Central Depository	KamAZ, Komineft, Transneft, Uralsviazinform
National Registry Company	Cheliabinsk Electrolytic Zinc Smelting Factory, St Petersburg Telephone, Lensviaz, LOMO, Novoship, Alfa cement, Norilsk Nickel, Northwest Shipping, Bee-Line (Vimpelcom)
NIKoil	LUKoil
Reestr-Service	Mosenergo
Reestr-Sviaz	Moscow City Telephone (will become registry for all regional telcos)

The main dilemma for the Russian market and many other frontier markets appears to be the consolidation of the different opinions on the future of a clearing and settlement organization: (1) NAUFOR (National Association of Securities Markets Participants) supports the creation of the Depository Clearing Company (DCC); (2) the MICEX (Moscow Interbank

---

[7] The company concerned was Elektrim. More information can be found in the Financial Times during the week of November 23rd, 1998.

Currency Exchange) which has adequate infrastructure in place for the clearing and settlement of currency and government securities transactions is promoting an equity clearing and settlement structure via the MICEX. This system is also supported by the Central Bank. (3) Recently the Federal Securities Commission on the Securities Market (FSCM) organized a new initiative which draws upon the participation of the Central Bank, the Ministry of Finance, issuers and market participants to create a new system-the Central Depository Working Group. The extent to which it differs from the Central Depository-Clearing Company (DCC) sponsored by NAUFOR, has not been established.

The question of shareholder registries has also not found its last answer. There are at least three opposing factions aiming at different outcomes in the creation of an efficient and reliable registration system: (1) regional governments support large local registries from which they could benefit as opposed to surrendering this process and the potential revenues to Moscow; (2) issuers still prefer pocket registries; (3) and finally the FCSM and most blue-chip issuers recognize the need for a National Registry Company.

III.B.3. Custody

Custody, which is the safekeeping of securities on behalf of their rightful owners, is an important element of the securities transaction and settlement process in pre-emerging markets. As most investors do not have branches or subsidiaries in the local pre-emerging markets, the availability of approved and trustworthy global custodian banks becomes vital to an efficient investment process.

In Russia, five local custodians qualified by 1998 as subcustodians under rule 17f-5 of the US Investment Companies Act. Subcustody relationships are formed with one of the five eligible subcustodians: Chase Manhattan, Credit Suisse, ABN Amro, Citibank, or Uneximbank, which all, except Uneximbank, must be backed by foreign parent companies with more than $200 million in shareholders' equity. Although, the growing number of 17f-5 qualified subcustodians has dramatically decreased the risks and obstacles associated with investing in Russian equities, the costs remain exorbitantly high. A typical transaction would involve a fee of $200 for the transfer of stock, or $20 for a book-entry transfer, expenses for travel to sometimes remote shareholder registries in Russia, a re-registration fee, an account opening fee, and monthly safe custody and administration fees.[8] This fee

---

[8] Brunswick Brokerage, "Infrastructure Update," (February 19, 1997): 6.

structure implies that the Russian market is virtually closed to retail investors. The introduction of the nominee-ownership option and the rapid rise of Moscow-based pooled registries has somewhat decreased the total expense incurred.

The age of *e-trade* and *Charles Schwab on-line,* when a complete transaction can cost as little as $8.95, has not reached Russia yet. However, given the relatively low infrastructure cost of such trading technology, one could foresee a leapfrogging of trading technology taking place in Russia or other frontier emerging markets in due time. Before this could happen, however, the establishment of a Russian Central Depository, which would qualify as an eligible 17f-5 custodian, would be necessary. Currently, the Depository Clearing Corporation (DCC) is in the process of testing a system that was has developed with NAUFOR for clearing and settling trades over the Russian Trading System (RTS).[9]

III.B.4. The Russian Trading System (RTS) and National Association of Securities Markets Participants (NAUFOR)

The most important and the most successful development in the Russian equity market has been the creation of the Russian Trading System (RTS). The RTS was founded in July 1995 by 12 Moscow-based brokers, organized under the umbrella organization of the Professional Association of Securities Market Participants (PAUFOR). PAUFOR was created to accelerate the progress in creating efficiency in the existing trading infrastructure. It was a self-regulated organization which took on the burden of fostering discipline, transparency, and order in the Russian equity market during a time when official bodies were not in the position to contribute to this process.

The most remarkable progress of the RTS, which links the regional markets and brokers into a unified trading network, has been the quickly diminishing degree of spreads between bid and ask quotes. Before 1995, the average spread was no less than 25%. In 1996 the average spread was in the range of 7%, and in mid-1997 the average spread was no more than 2%, which is comparable to more mature emerging markets. While this has been one of the primary accomplishments of the RTS, which delivers average bids and asks from the participating brokers and distributes the prices over an electronic network, it has also been a function of the rising investor interest in the frontier markets such as Russia. When the Russian equity market

---

[9] Brad Durham, "Coming of Age," *The Russian,* (July-August 1997): 24.

collapsed in August 1998, the narrowing trend in bid and ask spreads reversed sharply, which fully reflected the withdrawal of foreign investors and the reduced liquidity of local institutions.

The RTS currently consists of over 450 members (brokers, dealers, and banks) from the National Association of Securities Markets Participants (NAUFOR) covering ten time zones of the Russian Federation. The instruments traded are exclusively equities, and all shares are dematerialized and registered. The RTS consists of two tiers, first and second tier stocks, RTS-1 and RTS-2. RTS-1 must have a minimum daily trading volume of USD 100,000 and RTS-2 must have a minimum daily trading volume of USD 50,000. In 1997 there were 62 RTS-1 companies, and 88 RTS-2 companies listed. The RTS is an electronic quote-driven system, which in its structure is modeled on the NASDAQ. Brokers and market makers' quotes are displayed on the RTS screens, and trading is primarily conducted via telephone. RTS-1 companies have a minimum trading lot of USD 10,000 and RTS-2 companies have a minimum trading lot of USD 5,000. Margin trading, short selling, and block trading are not regulated. For hourly live prices and volumes of the RTS-1 and RTS-2 the homepage of the Russian Trading system is the most current and reliable source of information:

http://www.rtsnet.ru/rts/lasthour.htm

One must take into consideration that only trades among NAUFOR participants are fed into the RTS system, thus transactions in international depository receipts (ADRs or GDRs) are not conducted via the RTS and their volumes will not be reflected in chart 3.1 and chart 3.2. Furthermore, it is estimated that only 40%-50% of all transactions are captured by the RTS given that transactions among non-NAUFOR members and between NAUFOR and non-NAUFOR members are not registered under the RTS. Nevertheless, the RTS remains the most reliable indicator of prices and volume.

Chart 3.1. Russian Trading System (RTS-1) first tiers' trading volume

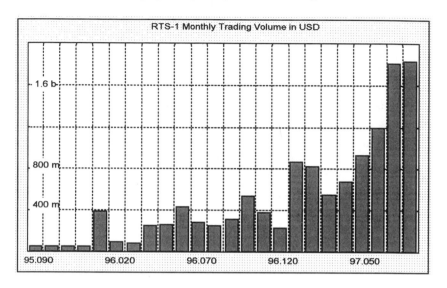

Chart 3.2. Russian Trading System (RTS-2) second tiers' trading volume

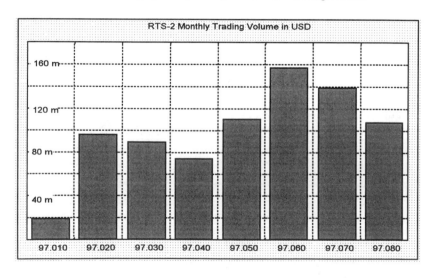

III.B.5.   Taxation and foreign investment approval

One of the developments in which many frontier markets are lagging behind the progress in political, economic and market formation, is fiscal policy in the investment area. Ill-designed or grossly asymmetric tax rules favoring foreign or local investors often lead to a structurally inadequate trading environment. In other cases, the absence of clearly defined rules leads to the development of potent off-shore trading centers capable of draining liquidity from the local market and thus slowing the capital market development and the financial disintermediation process locally. This can leave local banks in a more powerful position than necessary, and hinder the emergence of local capital market transparency. It also slows down the rise of a popular equity culture in the pre-emerging market as liquidity and trading takes place in the global ADR markets, or off-shore centers which are beyond reach for the average potential 'citizen' equity investor. Hence, policy makers in pre-emerging equity markets are well-advised to ensure that the infrastructure and legal framework is adequate to attract foreign investors not only to the equities operating in the local market, but also to transact within the legal boundaries of the local market.

In the case of Russian legislation during the early phase of the equity market emergence, the tax law had different effects on domestic and foreign investors. Unlike the case of many emerging markets, domestic investors (this includes the first Russian mutual funds) were clearly at an overall disadvantage compared to foreign investors. Returns achieved by domestic investors were taxed at the personal income tax rate which ranged from 12% to 35% depending in the income level of the investor. Russian legal entities were taxed at a flat rate of 35% and banks paid 43% in capital gains taxes. Furthermore, capital losses could not be offset against capital gains. This should explain why most wealthy Russians channeled their money via an offshore entity back into the Russian equity market.

Foreigners were required to pay the same rates. In practice, however, their tax rate was 0% as most cash was settled offshore. There was a 15% withholding tax on dividends, which in most cases was circumvented as many of the investment entities benefited from a favorable double taxation treaty with Cyprus.[10]

---

[10] Christodoulos Pelaghias, Seaward Intl., Cyprus, Harvard Univ. Russia Conference, Jan. 9-11, 1998, Cambridge, Massachusetts, panel discussion.

Box 3.0   Cyprus –Russian off-shore center

> Cyprus established itself as the location of choice for the Russian off-shore market. A double-taxation treaty, negotiated between the USSR and Cyprus at the peak of the Cold War in 1982, was intended to exclude Soviet government-controlled companies, which were set up to handle special tasks for the Communist government, from Cyprus taxation. Today, Cyprus is the official home of more than 40,000 off-shore companies of which close to 7,000 are Russian-owned. These include prominent names such as Inkombank, Menatep Bank, and many investment funds. Although the double taxation treaty has been challenged and continues to be challenged, even in 1999, as it facilitates tax evasion mechanisms, no conclusion has been reached on the future fiscal relationship between Russia and Cyprus. The costs of potentially cutting off large flows of funds from entering Russia via Cyprus-registered companies has to be balanced against the benefits of creating barriers for easy evasion of taxes. Tax evasion, however, is widely recognized as a domestic problem which cannot be solved by eliminating the legal conduit of Cyprus.
>
> Another development affecting the role of Cyprus as a Russian off-shore location is the negotiation between Cyprus and the European Union regarding Cyprus' accession to the EU. Under such an outcome, existing tax advantages may no longer be available. The time horizon on this development and the precedent of Ireland and Luxembourg, however, leave ample room for speculation on what in fact will happen to the tax legislation if Cyprus joins the EU in 3 to 5 years.

III.B.6.   Accounting peculiarities in frontier equity markets

The shortfalls of accounting transparency and comparability with IAS (International Accounting Standards) is a common phenomenon in most frontier emerging markets. The problems are more severe in those markets where there is no history of maintaining accounts for financial information and budgeting, but rather for purposes of government control and central planning. Accounting and interpretation of accounting items in frontier emerging markets, if taken seriously, is a vast area of knowledge requiring historical and cultural insight into economic management and often an understanding of the intricate mechanics of central planning. There are no universally applicable guidelines for all pre-emerging markets. There are, however, a number of simple rules and phenomena which tend to occur in most frontier markets that are emerging from the shadows of a centrally-planned economy.

As this book will later point out, understanding the accounting intricacies in frontier markets is not quintessential to understanding the market or to making profitable investment decisions. Nevertheless, the Russian case lends itself well to illustrating some of the prevailing themes in frontier emerging market accounting.[11]

Russian Accounting Rules (RAR) have traditionally served the purpose of informing Gosplan (the central planning agency) about quantities produced and flows of goods in the economy and the COMECON trading system. This book-keeping legacy is still felt as RAR primarily serve the tax authorities as opposed to assessing quantitatively the financial situation of the firm. Although RAR have undergone some change in the past three years, starting with the July 1994 'Accounting Policy Regulation Number One,' which implemented most IAS (International Accounting Standards) principles, there are still caveats in RAR of which the investor should be aware. Besides the imperfections, there are still numerous companies which have not fully adapted to the changes required.

While there is a growing number of financial statements created by Western auditors, according to IAS or even US GAAP, the guidelines for converting RAR into IAS or US GAAP are often not consistent across the different accounting firms. This makes financial statements prepared on the basis of RAR somewhat valuable for the analyst of Russian equities, given that comparability across Russian companies in RAR is not an option when using IAS statements prepared by different accounting firms. In practice, however, this exercise is rarely performed as only a small number of analysts of Russian equities have sufficient knowledge of the intricacies of RAR, and hence must rely on the short-dated history of IAS statements .

The most obvious differences between IAS and RAR can be outlined as follows:

---

[11] For a detailed analysis of Russian accounting and the implication for Western investors refer to: "Russian Accounting Beyond the Abacus," Nick Page, Paribas, October 1998.

Bad debts:

There are no uniform provision guidelines for bad debt. The regulation that Russian firms can only write-off bad debt after claiming bad debt for a minimum of a three-year time period, did not lead to creating provisions at a timely point when debt, under prudent accounting standards, was deemed to be non-collectible. This is slowly changing as companies are increasingly creating bad debt provisions when they realize the difference between accounting and taxable profit.

Fixed Assets:

The revaluation of fixed assets is obligatory on January 1 of each year. The government has created indexation guidelines for over 100 different assets classes, which is an improvement to the 'back-of-the-envelope' approach revaluation indices used before. Nevertheless, a full basket of exceptions is still available, particularly for oil and utility firms, which would excessively overstate their assets if revaluation took place according to the official guidelines. Those exceptions must be taken into consideration when analyzing the NAV of specific firms.

Depreciation:

Depreciation is more often than not understated as the depreciation schedule frequently assumes a longer asset life than prudent accounting would justify. However, the shorter depreciation schedule may still lead to an understatement if the assets had been excessively understated through opaque revaluation procedures. Thus both elements have to be considered when analyzing depreciation charges.

Profit/Loss Statement:

Accrual accounting principles have been introduced since the end of 1995, and an increasing number of companies abide by this rule. Comparisons over time, however, remain difficult, given that not all financial statements have been restated according to accrual accounting principles. The other problem is posed by the valuation of payments received that come in barter form (very often the case for utilities or engineering companies). Barter payments account for as much as 40% of total sales at some firms. The barter goods are valued according to what the two parties involved agree upon, as opposed to fair market value. This has been a problem as many companies associate 'political' terms with the barter deal. Other distortions are caused by the omission of certain items from cost of goods sold (COGS) These items, which would otherwise reduce taxable income, are instead categorized as 'transfer to reserves.' Such items include social costs, fines for late tax payments, pollution fines, etc.

Consolidated Statements:

This is still a large gray area in RAR as many companies do not consolidate accounts, or only do so imperfectly.[12]

Generally, accounting information has not been very conclusive when analyzing Russian companies. As more Russian companies aspire to list on international exchanges, which requires IAS and US GAAP statements, there will be a growing number of companies which will also have a three year history of IAS and/or US GAAP financial statements. In the meantime, and for the remaining companies that are lagging in transparent financial reporting, the analyst often has to think around corners and question the obvious. For example, the fact that companies own and operate schools, kindergartens and social facilities, and list them on their balances sheets as assets could imply that such assets require cash outflows and thus have a negative net present value (NPV) associated with them. Furthermore, a fair market value of social infrastructure is not easy to estimate as there are not too many potential buyers for a run-down nursery installed during the 1950s for children of parents working in the factory.

III.C. A snapshot of current problems affecting the equity market valuation of Russia

At the beginning of 1998, before the currency collapse in the fall of 1998, the Russian market had reached a new level of interest. The question arose of why Russian blue chips were still trading at a discount to comparable blue

---

[12] Useful comments on Russian accounting rules can be found in:
"Handle with Care: Selected Topics in Russian Accounting," *Morgan Stanley Dean Witter-Emerging Markets Investment Research* (3 June 1997): 6-9.
"Russia Coming in from the Cold," *Flemings Research* (August 1996): 84-85.
"Russian Equity Guide," *Brunswick Brokerage* (1995): 11-12.

chips in other emerging markets, such as Brazil or Mexico.[13] The reason for this discount was primarily found in the inadequate equity market infrastructure. As of early 1998, the Russian market still lacked many fundamental mechanisms and legal rules that are required for a first-rate emerging market:

(a) The lack of a centralized clearing mechanism still carries the risk of companies erasing their shareholders from the company share register. Trades have to be hand-settled by brokers. This could lead to long delays and a paper crisis under increased volumes.

(b) The lack of a central clearing house often shuts out smaller brokerages as the larger brokerages assess the risk of their default as too high.

(c) The capital gains tax law for foreigners still deters foreigners from moving with their trading activity on-shore. This leads to a segregated market where foreigners trade with each other off-shore and local banks (which are only allowed to transact on-shore and in rubles) remain on-shore. This situation has given rise to the notion that "the market is filled with dollar sellers but only ruble buyers."[14]

(d) Shareholder rights are still unsatisfactorily enforced. While there are companies that take minority shareholders' interests seriously, such as LUKoil or Mosenergo, others, such as Yukos still pursue top management interests at the cost of minority shareholders, often without legal consequences.

Assessing the Russian market, or for that matter other pre-emerging markets, therefore becomes a direct function of not only the micro-level analysis of companies (which will be examined at a later point in this study), or macro-economic fundamentals, but also function of the equity market infrastructure, from which no single company can be isolated. To monitor

---

[13] The discount is expressed by substantially lower P/E multiples (up to 60%) compared to Brazilian or Mexican stocks in the same industry and similar liquidity-enhancement instruments in place (ADRs) –(pre-crisis numbers in early 1998).

[14] Harvey Sawikin, "The Russian Stock Market: First-Rank or Second-Rate? *The Russian* (December/January 1998): 24-25.

the progress or setbacks in such a process becomes crucial when gauging a widening or narrowing valuation gap between Russia and other emerging markets. Hence, the market infrastructure dimension is one of the most powerful equity valuation drivers in frontier equity markets.

Chapter 4

Data and Descriptive Features of a Frontier Equity Market

Frontier markets in the statistical twilight zone

This chapter has three main purposes: (a) to describe the data set used in the analysis, (b) to assess the probability distribution of the time series of individual Russian equities, and (c) to examine the properties of the return-volatility trade-off (mean-variance frontiers) as it evolves over time. Particularly, the underlying probability distribution properties are noteworthy as the methodology used for assessing the relative degree of market efficiency in a later chapter is selected to be consistent with the probability distribution observed in Russian equities.

The emergence of on-line technology, which at virtually no cost can distribute live price and other market-relevant information, has drastically altered the approach to data gathering for emerging markets. This study exploits the advantage of electronically-readable data distributed via the internet. Moreover, the availability of live on-line information services has dramatically decreased the infrastructure cost of operating an asset management company trading securities from the most exotic places. This is a process, which in itself should have an impact on market efficiency and global financial integration. Given that an increasing number of asset management firms trading the Russian market, or other frontier emerging equity markets rely exclusively on low or no-cost web sites for their daily business information, the sources of data presented are deemed to be reliable.

IV.A.   Descriptive statistics of Russian securities

IV.A.1. Data sources and selection of Russian securities

The set of securities presented in table 4.0. was selected for the Russian frontier market case study as it reflects the composition of the broader Russian equity market. A heavy concentration in natural resource stocks, particularly in oil and gas, followed by electric utilities and telecommunication companies form the core of the equity universe for investors. Limited availability of reliable data for securities other than those presented in table 4.0. did not allow for their inclusion.

The most reliable and accurate historical time series of Russian equity prices available to the public are provided by RinacoPlus, one of Russia's more prominent brokerages during the heyday of the Russian equity market in 1996 and 1997. RinacoPlus, in order to preserve consistency with its initial methodology averaged best bids and asks at the close of the RTS (6:00pm Moscow time). Bids and asks are sourced from the RTS, or if liquidity does not allow usage of the RTS, the AK&M database.[1] Dividends are not considered as virtually no dividend payments were made for most of the time span analyzed, and even today only a small number of companies pay only token amounts of dividends. Only domestic prices are used, which means that ADR prices are not included. ADR prices are quoted over the counter of global brokerages and are thus not *reliably* available. Daily data points of prices are used to obtain a sizable data sample. When using daily data points, the assumption of equi-distance is violated, this however, has to be taken into account as longer time intervals would not allow for meaningful sample sizes. All prices quoted on the RTS are denominated in US dollars, the currency in which trading is conducted. All time series used in the analysis are available under:

http//www.fe.msk.ru/infomarket/rinacoplus/indicat/metod.html#3

---

[1] Prices used in this study are from securities where reliance on AK&M will not be necessary as all securities are traded on the RTS-1. For a discussion on the merits of using bid/ask averages over closing prices refer to the Fisher effect (Fisher 1966).

Table 4.0. Securities Description

Ticker	Company Name	Sector	Market Capitalization (in m $)[2]
EESR	Unified Energy Systems	Utility	18,092
MSNG	Mosenergo	Utility	3,967
IRGZ	Irkutskenergo	Utility	1,655
LENE	Lenenergo	Utility	865
LKOH	LUKoil	Oil/Gas	16,928
YFGA	Yuganskneftegas	Oil/Gas	1,809
SNGS	Surgutneftegas	Oil/Gas	7,317
PFGS	Purneftegas	Oil/Gas	892
MFGS	Megionnneftegas	Oil/Gas	1,250
NYGS	Noyabrskneftegas	Oil/Gas	1,241
TOMG	Tomskneft	Oil/Gas	936
NZGZ	Nizhnevartovskneftegas	Oil/Gas	683
CHGS	Chornogorneft	Oil/Gas	313
OREB	Orenburgneft	Oil/Gas	n/a
GAZP	Gazprom	Oil/Gas	16,453
RTKM	Rostelekom	Telecom	4,631
SPTL	St Petersburg Telephone	Telecom	1,224
MGTS	MGTS Telecom	Telecom	3,043
GUMM	Trade House GUM	Retail	253

[2] Market Capitalization as of July 31, 1997.

Ticker	*Company Name*	*Sector*	*Market Capitalization (in m $)[3]*
NKEL	Norilsk Nickel	Mining	1,928
KMAZ	Kamaz	Autos	407
GAZA	Gaz Auto Plant	Autos	480
FESH	FESC	Shipping	115

Source: AK&M, RTS

IV.A.2. The probability distribution of individual shares

The probability distribution of returns in emerging markets has been assessed in a number of studies.[4] Normality has been rejected for most studies on emerging market indices.[5] This section examines the distribution properties of individual Russian equities.

Table 4.1. indicates the rejection of the normality assumption for every security examined.[6] Excess positive kurtosis seems to prevail, and the leptokurtic state of the distribution indicates a slim or long tailed distribution. Most of the securities also display positive skewness, which implies a distribution to the right.

[3] Market Capitalization as of July 31, 1997.
[4] Refer to the following two studies for further details: Geert Bakaert, "Market integration and investment barriers in emerging equity markets," *World Bank Economic Review* 9 (1995): 75-107.
Geert Bakaert and Campbell R. Harvey, "Emerging equity market volatility," forthcoming.
[5] For evidence of rejection of normality in emerging markets see Hakim (1992) and Claessens, Dasgupta, Glen (1993). The likelihood that an index is more 'well-behaved' than individual securities further supports the notion that the normality assumption in individual emerging market securities can be rejected.

[6] The Jarque-Bera test statistic follows the chi-square distribution with 2 df. There are a number of reasons why normality can be rejected. Refer to Black (1976), Christie (1982), Nelson(1991), and Brennan (1993) for detailed discussions of topics such as presence of limited liability in equity investments, option-like asymmetry in index returns, or conditional skewness -Harvey and Siddique (1995).

Table 4.1. Descriptive Statistics (daily observations)

Company	Mean	Std. Dev.	Sharpe Ratio	Kurtosis	Skewness	JB
EESR	0.41%	3.66%	0.107	5.72	0.62	245
LENE	0.42%	3.42%	0.117	18.99	2.03	7458
YFGA	0.15%	3.96%	0.032	9.90	1.15	1451
SNGS	0.34%	4.89%	0.065	8.53	0.99	944
PFGS	0.24%	3.82%	0.058	8.46	0.70	870
MFGS	0.27%	4.45%	0.057	6.26	0.56	325
NYGS	0.17%	3.67%	0.040	10.23	1.14	1578
TOMG	0.23%	3.82%	0.055	8.50	0.52	858
NZGZ	0.28%	5.41%	0.048	73.10	5.63	138210
CHGZ	0.18%	3.30%	0.047	15.82	0.86	4591
ORNB	0.35%	5.32%	0.061	12.12	0.85	2361
GAZP	0.42%	5.35%	0.075	12.57	1.01	2625
RTKM	0.34%	3.61%	0.087	7.83	0.90	728
SPTL	0.26%	2.82%	0.083	11.85	-0.11	2150
MGTS	0.43%	2.72%	0.149	62.23	4.56	98157
GUMM	0.16%	4.38%	0.031	269.72	-12.23	1966749
NKEL	0.09%	3.65%	0.018	8.04	0.73	756
KMAZ	0.20%	5.37%	0.034	15.45	0.86	4329
GAZA	0.61%	5.43%	0.108	21.27	1.49	9400
LKOH	0.25%	2.98%	0.077	7.62	0.86	665
IRGZ	0.44%	4.18%	0.100	7.27	0.81	573
MSNG	0.43%	3.34%	0.123	7.17	0.67	527
FESH	0.14%	5.08%	0.024	53.60	3.30	71383
AVERAGE	0.30%	4.11%	0.07	28.79	0.78	100749

Source: RTS, Nov. 1995 -March 1998.

The average returns distribution of those Russian equities presented above, can be graphically described as more peaked (leptocurtic) and more heavily clustered to the left of the mean (skewed to the right).

Diagram 4.0.   Graphical illustration of Russian equity returns distribution

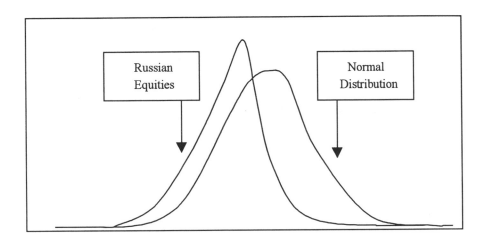

Particularly noteworthy is that those equities with the highest trading volume (Unified Energy Systems, Mosenergo, Irkutskenergo, LUKoil, and Rostelekom) have comparatively the most 'well-behaved' Jarque-Bera normality scores.   This could indicate that active trading fosters an increasingly normal distribution of returns.

Nevertheless, the conclusion from the fact that we observe deviation from the normal distribution, requires the application of a methodology which is robust to non-normality when measuring relative market efficiency in chapter 6. The safest method would be to simply use non-parametric methods. However, given the shortfalls of such tests (as discussed in chapter 2), the variance ratio test appears to be a sound choice. MacKinlay and Lo (1988) state in their original article on the variance ratio test, that this test is sensitive to correlated price changes, but otherwise robust to many forms of non-normality and heteroscedasticity, and thus lends itself well to the analysis of financial time series which often deviate from normality.

Excursion – *Definition of statistical measures*:

Mean: The mean is calculated as the average daily USD return for the time period from January 1995 to September 1997.

Standard deviation: The standard deviation is calculated according to the conventional formula and represents the daily standard deviation (not annualized).

Sharpe Ratio: The Sharpe Ratio is computed in unconventional terms as the average daily risk free rate is subtracted from the average daily return before it is divided by the daily standard deviation (daily frequency).[7] The Sharpe ratio measures the risk premium earned per unit of risk exposure. Thus, a higher Sharpe ratio is preferable to a lower Sharpe ratio. This could be a result of lower volatility of the underlying asset, or higher return.

Skewness and Kurtosis: Skewness and kurtosis measure the characteristics of the returns distribution. Positive skewness implies that the distribution is tilted to the right, negative skewness to the left, and zero skewness implies symmetry about its mean, such as the normal distribution. Kurtosis provides a measure of the weight in the tail of a probability density function. For a normal distribution the population kurtosis is 3.

$$Skewness = \frac{\sum_{i=1}^{n}(X_i - \overline{X})^3 / n}{s^3}$$

$$Kurtosis = \frac{\sum_{i=1}^{n}(X_i - \overline{X})^4 / n}{s^4}$$

$$\overline{X} = sample...mean$$
$$s = sample..stdev.$$

Jarque-Bera Normality Test: The J.-B. test is an asymptotic (large sample) test, and as such it is based on OLS (ordinary least squares) residuals. The J.-B. test statistic follows the chi-square distribution at 2 df. Thus, if the J.-B. value is lower than the test statistic one cannot reject the normality assumption.[8]

---

[7] The Sharpe ratio is conventionally calculated only for longer time periods, but for the sake of comparison the daily frequency is maintained. The risk-free rate used is the USD rate because this study assumes the US investor's perspective.

[8] See M. Jarque and A.K. Bera, "A Test for Normality of Observations and Regression Residuals," *International Statistical Review*, vol. 55 (1987): 163-172.

$$J.B.= n\left[\frac{(Skewness)^2}{6} + \frac{(Kurtosis-3)^2}{24}\right]$$

IV.B. Mean-variance frontier

The mean-variance frontier serves to illustrate the trade-off between volatility and return. Traditionally, the mean-variance frontier reflects investors' preference for lower volatility at the cost of lower return, or vice versa. This is also one of the underlying premises of the Capital-Asset Pricing Model (CAPM). Under CAPM, the risk-adjusted expected returns of all securities are equal and any differences across assets in expected rates of return are due to unavoidable uncertainty, which is captured in historical volatility of the asset versus its market portfolio.[9] While the CAPM uses the covariance of a security with the market portfolio (also called beta) as a risk measure, as opposed to simply using variance, the assumption remains the same: Higher expected returns require higher expected uncertainty. Therefore, we must assume that investors are concerned with the volatility of their assets. In developed markets this is fairly well presented. Simple examples such as semiconductor or biotechnology stocks as compared to the Mid-western sewage utility, serve as good examples of the high volatility and high return / low volatility and low return trade-off.

Pre-emerging market equities in the Russian market do not fit into this return/volatility school of thought. Chart 4.0. shows the mean-variance frontier for the time period between January 1995 and September 1997 for twenty-three of Russia's most liquid equities measured by their cumulative RTS trading volume between January and June of 1997. Chart 4.1. also depicts a mean-variance frontier for the same set of Russian equities, but the time interval measured is limited to the twelve months period ranging from September 1996 to September 1997. Chart 4.1. has been plotted to test for

[9] Robert A. Haugen. *Modern Investment Theory.* 4th ed. Upper Saddle River, NJ, Prentice Hall: 1997, chapter 7 passim.

the possibility of the mean-variance frontier of a maturing Russian equity market approaching the traditional risk-return trade-off relationship observed in mature markets or other emerging markets.[10]

As one can see, however, the traditional risk-return trade-off does not hold true in Russia. The linear fit line does not exhibit an upward slope.[11] In fact, the slope is slightly negative. This leads to the realization that more volatile securities generate lower returns. Interestingly, the upper-left quarter (higher return/ lower volatility) of the chart has a fairly high concentration of the most liquid stocks (MSNG, UES-EESR, RTKM, MGTS). This is possibly an indicator that securities with lower liquidity, which attract less foreign investment, are less exposed to liquidity-surges in their stocks price (hence lower returns) and are more vulnerable to dramatic fluctuations (hence higher volatility) given a relatively lower liquidity.

This somewhat forced line of argumentation tries to apply sense and reason to the observations in chart 4.0. A more reasonable interpretation of chart 4.0, however, is that investors are not concerned with volatility, and that the slightly negative slope is more coincidence than a reflection of some underlying mechanism prevailing. The question arises of whether investors in pre-emerging markets such as Russia are volatility-sensitive given the fact that even the least volatile assets have an annualized standard deviation of 30%-40%. Furthermore, it can be safely assumed that foreign investors are far more concerned with more fundamental risks, such as political collapse or expropriation, than short-term volatility.

The more recent twelve month time period does not exhibit a trend delineating a closer resemblance with a traditional risk-return trade-off assumption either, although the exclusion of the Far Eastern Shipping Company (FESH) and Trade House Gum (GUMM) would lead to a positive slope. This would indicate a movement towards the more traditional risk-return trade off assumption. Nevertheless, it still can be concluded that the Russian market remains a stock pickers' market, where risk and return are not providing an indifference curve, and where high risk is not necessarily associated with higher return or vice-versa.

---

[10] Stijn Claessens; Sasmita Dasgupta; and Jack Glen, "Stock Price Behavior in Emerging Markets," *World Bank Discussion Series on Emerging Stock Markets* (1996): 304.

[11] The linear fit was chosen as OLS (ordinary least squares) would not have been the most efficient representation due to the non-fulfillment of the normality assumption in the data set.

Chart 4.0. Mean Variance Frontier of Russian Equities (1995-1997)[12]

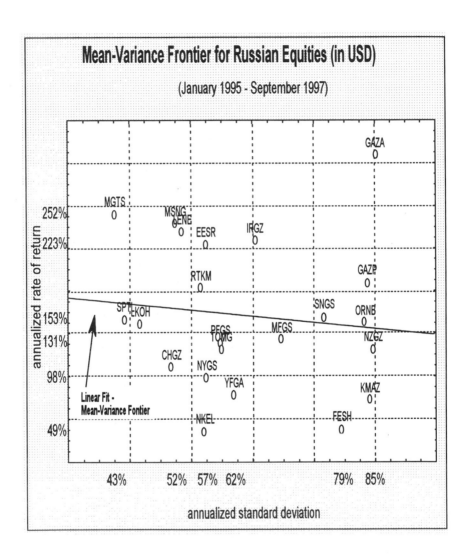

[12] The rates of return have been annualized from daily frequency observations and the daily standard deviation has been annualized by multiplying it by the square root of 245.

Chart 4.1. Mean Variance Frontier of Russian Equities (96 – Sep 97)

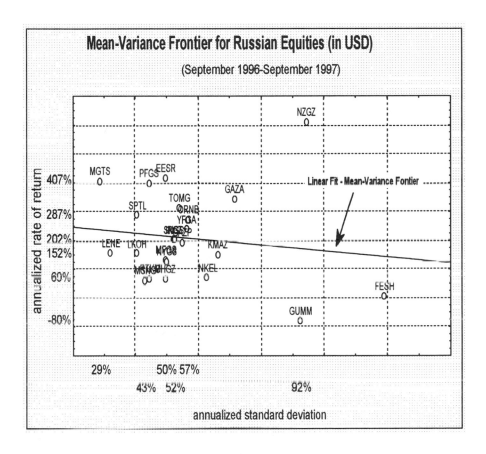

The most recent time period of chart 4.2. allows for analysis of a larger universe of Russian equities (35). Here one can see that volatility and return increasingly become positively correlated, thus contributing to the assumption that the Russian market is increasingly analyzed with volatility in mind and other risks are taking a less prevalent place in the hierarchy of measures. Hence, a closer integration of the Russian market in global capital markets could be inferred from such an observation. Furthermore, the overall volatility decreases in chart 4.2. compared to chart 4.0., which also suggests Russia is gradually and steadily adapting to the volatility profile of more mature emerging markets.

Chart 4.2. Mean Variance Frontier of Russian Equities (96 – Sep 97)

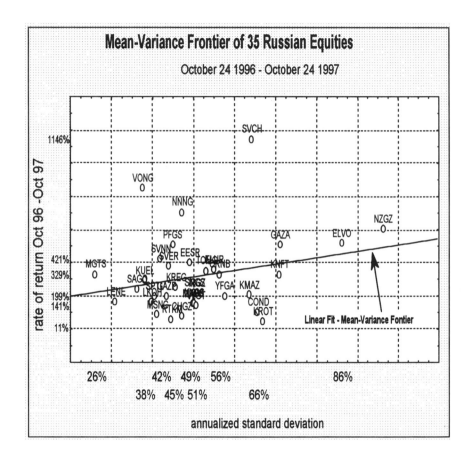

Chapter 5

Information Channels in Frontier Emerging Markets
Building informational efficiency

Informational efficiency can only exist to the degree to which information about individual companies reaches the investor. This chapter raises the question: How do foreign investors learn about the pre-emerging stock market of Russia and its companies? After establishing that the main channel of information is brokerage research reports, a more detailed analysis is conducted about individual companies and their transparency in light of this predominant information channel. Finally, three portfolios are created: (1) top-transparency portfolio, (2) medium-transparency portfolio, and (3) bottom-transparency portfolio. The creation of the three portfolios is supported by the AK&M survey which ranks companies by their degree of information disclosure.[1] The three portfolios will be used in chapter 7 as a prerequisite for the comparative analysis of relative market efficiency.

V.A. Informational channels and brokerage research coverage index

V.A.1. Information channels of security information on Russian equities

Emerging markets are never as transparent as developed markets, and indeed, greater transparency is the hallmark of the emergence process.

---

[1] The AK&M quarterly survey can be retrieved from AK&M's web site (www.akm.ru). AK&M has established itself as one of the most authoritative firms delivering market quotes and industry indices in Russia-not unlike Standard & Poor's SP500, or Dow Jones & Co.'s DJIA in the US.

Information about securities in pre-emerging markets such as Russia, however, has been even less accessible to foreign investors. This is particularly true during the initial stages in the development of a securities market. Financial statement projections, reliable audits, a clear overview of company operations and ownership structure, or strategic outlook are just a few of the desirable pieces of information that are often insufficiently available in pre-emerging markets. In the absence of this market information, one must question what information is actually used as a basis for investment decision-making.[2]

The purpose of this chapter is to assess what the main channels of information are and what the implications are for individual securities' transparency and investor appeal. Such a question could be considered unanswerable in any developed market, where sector rotations and strategic outlook fine-tuning, to name just a few criteria, are continuously reshuffling the securities appeal profiles and their relative visibility levels on the investor radar screen. In young emerging markets, however, the question is quite simple: What information is available to the foreign investor and how can one measure the scarce and only information offered to foreign investors?

To gain an insight into the information channels of pre-emerging market investors in the Russian equities market, the following three types of analyses will be shared. In 1996, the ICR Survey Research Group conducted a survey of 174 Western portfolio investors in Russia on behalf of the Federal Commission on the Russian Capital Market.[3] This survey, in addition to the AK&M quarterly surveys, dating back to 1994, which polls 400 market participants on issuers' information disclosure and general securities appeal, complement the analysis of research coverage of individual Russian issuers, which is conducted in this study.

As one can see from the ICR survey results on chart 5.0. and chart 5.1., Western investors participating in the Russian equity market rely on brokers'

---

[2] A good introduction to investment channel analysis for global equity markets is given by:
W. Scott Bauman, "Channels used to research global equity investments," *The Journal of Investing*, vol. 5, no.4 (Winter 1996): 37-46. In other pre-emerging markets, the channels of information are likely to be the same as in Russia. Some of the smaller pre-emerging markets, particularly in sub-Saharan Africa, however, cannot rely to the same degree on brokerage research as the resulting deal flow - in underwriting and trading - is not expected to be very large. Consequently brokerage research resources are allocated to larger markets.

[3] Survey can be obtained from ICR Survey Research Group- AUS Consultants, Media, PA 19565-9280.

research reports (49%) as their main source of Russian capital market information. Other fairly unspecialized publications such as the *Financial Times* or *The Economist* also serve as an important source of information for Russian market participants, accounting for 19% and 17%, respectively. In the category 'other', the on-line information services Reuters and Bloomberg stand out as the most important sources of information.

These results clearly indicate that brokers' research reports should be the best indicator of an individual company's visibility in the investment community. On-line information tends to be quite specific to events affecting a company, or alternatively, fairly general when it pertains to overall conditions in the country and investor sentiment.

Chart 5.0. Information channels for Russian investors

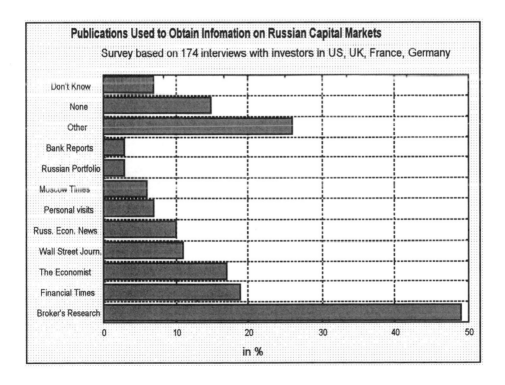

The same is valid for the *Financial Times* and *The Economist*, both of which have ad-hoc journalistic coverage of industries or Russian political events, but do not display the continuity and detail that investors need in order to make decisions. Hence, the best measure of transparency remains the traditional brokerage research report on companies.

Chart 5.1. Information channels for Russian investors

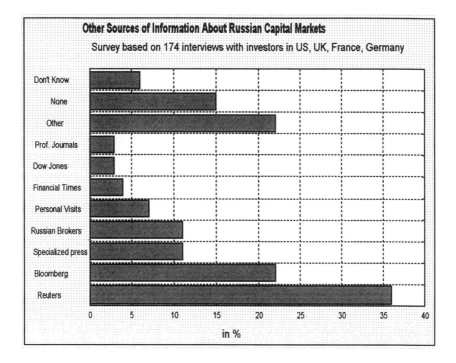

V.A.2. Brokerage report coverage index

Given that brokerage research reports are the most widely used sources of information for pre-emerging market decision-makers, a complete account of brokerage research has been established covering the time span between January 1995 and September 1997 in Russia.

The information was obtained via four main routes:

1. mail delivery of reports to buy-side analyst,
2. posting of reports on on-line database FirstCall Research Direct,
3. survey of brokerages sent out via e-mail,
4. Russia Portfolio publications printed research review in quarterly intervals including all of the above mentioned brokers.

The following brokerages have been included in establishing the transparency/investor appeal index:

Table 5.0. Brokerages included in survey

BROKERAGE NAME	BROKERAGE NAME
Alfa Capital	Merrill Lynch
Aton	Morgan Stanley Dean Witter
Brunswick Brokerage	Paribas/United Financial Group
CentreInvest Securities	Pioneer Securities
Credit Suisse First Boston	Prospect Investment
Daiwa	Renaissance Capital
Deutsche Morgan Grenfell	Rinaco Plus
ING Barings	Rye, Man & Gore
Lentroimeterialy	Salomon Smith Barney
MC-BBL	Sector Capital
MFK-Bank	Troika Dialog

The information obtained from each brokerage included the date, the company, and the recommendation of each report written on a Russian security, or an industry report comprising several securities. If the recommendation was positive, neutral or negative (many brokerages did not release recommendations in the first phase of their coverage), the coverage was counted as a one. Interestingly, there were not too many sell recommendations until the later phase of the period observed. The total score per company was then cumulatively tracked on a monthly basis.

Cumulative counting seems justifiable in light of the fact that buy-side analysts mostly receive a package containing all of the research that has been published by individual brokerages when inquiring about information on a specific company in a pre-emerging market. Furthermore, cumulative counting supports the notion that analysts create a latent memory for the visibility of certain companies if research reports have come through their desks in the past.

Table 5.1. Cumulative brokerage report coverage

	GAZP	NZGZ	NYGS	MFGS	ORNB	TOMG	LKOH	CHGZ	YFGA	SNGS	PFGS	UES	LEN	MSNG	IRGZ	MGTS	SPTL	RTKM	GUMM	KMAZ	GAZA	FESH	NKEL
95/1	0	0	0	0	0	0	0	0	0	0	0	0	0	0	0	0	0	0	0	0	0	0	0
95/2	1	1	1	1	0	1	2	1	0	1	1	2	0	0	0	1	2	2	0	0	0	0	2
95/3	1	2	2	2	1	2	3	2	1	2	2	2	0	0	0	1	2	2	0	0	0	0	2
95/4	2	3	3	3	2	3	5	3	2	3	3	3	1	1	1	2	3	3	0	1	1	1	3
95/5	2	3	4	4	2	3	6	3	2	4	3	3	1	1	1	2	3	3	0	1	1	1	3
95/6	2	3	4	4	2	3	7	4	2	5	3	3	1	1	2	3	4	5	0	1	1	1	3
95/7	2	3	4	4	2	3	7	4	2	5	3	3	1	1	2	3	4	6	0	1	1	2	3
95/8	2	3	4	4	2	3	7	4	2	5	3	3	1	1	2	4	5	6	0	1	1	2	3
95/9	2	3	4	4	2	3	8	4	2	5	3	3	1	3	2	4	5	7	0	1	1	2	3
95/10	2	3	4	4	2	3	8	4	2	5	3	4	1	3	2	4	5	7	0	1	1	2	3
95/11	2	3	4	4	2	3	8	4	2	5	3	4	1	3	2	4	5	7	0	1	1	2	3
95/12	2	3	4	4	2	3	8	4	2	5	3	4	1	3	2	4	5	7	0	1	1	2	3
96/1	2	3	4	4	2	3	9	4	2	5	3	4	1	4	2	4	5	7	0	1	1	2	3
96/2	2	3	4	4	2	3	10	4	2	5	3	4	1	4	2	4	5	8	0	1	1	2	3
96/3	2	4	5	5	3	4	13	6	2	7	4	4	1	5	2	4	5	8	0	2	1	2	4
96/4	2	4	6	7	3	4	16	6	2	8	4	6	2	6	4	4	5	8	1	2	2	3	5
96/5	3	5	7	8	4	5	15	7	2	9	5	8	3	9	7	4	5	8	1	2	3	3	5
96/6	4	6	8	9	6	6	17	10	4	11	6	9	3	11	7	6	7	10	1	3	3	4	5
96/7	5	6	9	11	5	7	19	11	4	12	6	9	3	12	7	7	7	11	2	3	3	5	5
96/8	6	6	9	11	6	7	20	11	4	12	6	9	3	15	7	7	7	12	5	4	4	5	5
96/9	9	6	10	11	6	7	25	12	4	13	6	10	3	16	7	8	8	14	7	4	4	6	5
96/10	12	6	10	11	6	7	25	13	5	14	6	10	3	18	7	8	10	18	8	5	4	7	5
96/11	12	9	10	12	7	8	27	18	7	15	7	10	4	19	9	8	11	19	9	5	4	7	5
96/12	13	9	10	12	8	8	29	19	7	15	8	13	6	22	11	9	13	23	9	5	4	7	7
97/1	13	9	10	13	9	8	31	20	8	18	8	13	6	23	11	10	15	27	11	5	4	7	8
97/2	13	9	10	13	9	8	32	22	8	20	8	13	6	24	13	12	16	28	12	5	4	7	8
97/3	13	10	10	13	9	8	34	21	8	21	8	16	7	26	15	12	16	30	14	5	5	7	8
97/4	16	10	10	13	9	8	35	21	8	21	8	17	7	27	15	12	16	30	14	6	6	7	8
97/5	17	10	10	13	9	8	35	21	8	22	8	18	7	27	15	14	17	32	16	6	6	8	8
97/6	18	11	10	16	10	10	37	21	9	24	8	18	7	30	15	14	18	32	16	6	7	8	8
97/7	19	11	10	15	10	10	38	21	9	24	8	18	8	31	15	16	20	34	16	7	7	8	8
97/8	19	11	11	16	10	10	38	21	9	24	8	21	8	33	15	17	20	35	16	8	8	8	10
97/9	21	11	11	16	10	10	39	21	9	24	8	22	8	34	17	17	20	36	16	8	9	8	10

V.A.3. AK&M Survey

The AK&M Survey which polls over 400 market participants in quarterly intervals on their opinions about information disclosure of (a) individual securities, and (b) appeal of individual securities, sharply confirms the results that have been obtained through the above depicted transparency analysis in table 5.1. The top five portfolio is matched between 80%-100% by the quarterly survey results for the top five securities based on information disclosure. Furthermore, the information disclosure top five list is almost perfectly matched in each quarter by the same top five names in the 'securities appeal' poll.

This means, that (a) the brokerage report analysis is confirmed and, (b) that the degree of information disclosure directly translates into the degree of appeal that individual securities enjoy in the top ranking environment with regard to the individual criteria. The same comparison could not be conducted for the low end of information disclosure, brokerage reports and securities appeal, as the universe used by AK&M differs since it includes more illiquid names with little price history available and which hence were not considered for this analysis.

Table 5.2. AK&M Survey -top five stocks based on information disclosure

October 1, 1997	June 27, 1997	March 31, 1997	December 26, 1996	Sept 27, 1996
UES	UES	UES	UES	UES
LUKoil	LUKoil	LUKoil	LUKoil	LUKoil
Mosenergo	Mosenergo	Mosenergo	Mosenergo	Mosenergo
Rostelekom	Rostelekom	Rostelekom	Rostelekom	Rostelekom
Gazprom	Gazprom	Gazprom	Gazprom	Norilsk Nickel

June 28, 1996	Mar. 29, 1996	Dec. 29, 1995	Sept. 30, 1995	June 27, 1995
LUKoil	UES	UES	UES	UES
Mosenergo	LUKoil	Rostelekom	Rostelekom	Rostelekom
UES	Rostelekom	Norilsk Nickel	Norilsk Nickel	Norilsk Nickel
Rostelekom	Mosenergo	LUKoil	Yugansk.	Yugansk.
Norilsk Nickel	Norilsk Nickel	Mosenergo	LUKoil	LUKoil

V.A.4. Creation of top-, medium-, and bottom-transparency portfolios

The top-, medium-, and bottom-transparency portfolios for the full period
(January 1995 – September 1997) have been created by bundling the top five
stocks, the bottom five stocks, and the remainder in the middle, which
accounts for thirteen stocks, into three portfolios. The reason why the top
and the bottom portfolio are composed of only five securities is because the
top 'five group' has been quite consistent over the entire period. This could

not be said for the top 'six' or 'seven' group. Since the measurement of the random walk relative to securities transparency is applied to the whole period (660 trading days), a consistent top transparency group is desirable. The reason why Gazprom is not in the top transparency portfolio can be explained by the fact that Gazprom was not a company in which foreigners could invest until the October 1996 ADR issue. This is why international brokerages only took a marginal interest in the company and did not publish extensive research on the firm during the pre-ADR period.

As of June 1997, the market capitalization of the top transparency portfolio accounted for 45% (57% excluding Gazprom from total MSE market capitalization) of the total Moscow Stock Exchange (MSE) market capitalization.[4] This further supports the view that the top five selection is a reasonable choice as a sixth or seventh addition would only marginally increase the total market capitalization of the portfolio. A top five portfolio, on the other hand, consists of a homogenous group of highly capitalized and consequently more liquid companies that share many characteristics, particularly with regard to the appeal to foreign investors resulting from transparency.

Table 5.3.   Portfolio-transparency breakdown

Top Transparency	Bottom Transparency
LUKoil	Yuganskneftegas
Rostelekom	Lenenergo
Mosenergo	KAMAZ
Surgutneftegas	Far Eastern Shipping Company
Unified Energy Systems	Purneftegas

---

[4] Daiwa Securities, "Central/Eastern Europe-Moving in Different Orbits," *Daiwa Europe Limited Equity Strategy Quarterly* (June 1997): 30.

Table 5.3. Portfolio-transparency breakdown (continued)

Medium Transparency	
Gazprom	Chernogorneft
St. Petersburg Telecom	Irktutskenergo
MGTS (Telecom)	GUMM
Megionneftegas	Nizhnevartovskneftegas
Noyabrskneftegas	Norilsk Nickel
Orenburgneft	Tomskneft
Gaza Auto Plant	

Table 5.3. defines the three portfolios according to the transparency criteria of the companies composing the three portfolios. Securities in the top transparency portfolio are those that are on the forefront of information release to investors. This has two major implications: (1) investors know more about the company-specific details, and (2) more investors are aware of the existence of those securities than of those which belong to the other two portfolios. Accordingly, a double-edged sword situation may arise which is the consequence of market segmentation.

Given the higher visibility of the top transparency portfolio, a specific investor group is likely to be more attracted to those securities than to securities in the other two portfolios. At the same time, those securities composing the top transparency portfolio are on the forefront of delivering transparency. The implications for relative market efficiency will be the topic of chapter 7.

Chapter 7 will examine whether the top transparency portfolio, given its high information release characteristics, will confirm the common notion that higher transparency generates a higher degree of relative market efficiency. Or whether precisely those characteristics lead to the type of investor segmentation which could override the benefits of transparency. In theory that should translate into greater informational efficiency and thus a higher degree of relative market efficiency, but in reality this could possibly lead to a lower degree relative market efficiency. This is the train of arguments which opens the stage for the often underestimated effects of market segmentation theory, which in turn can be a result of behavioral finance, or sometimes simply practical investment necessities and requirements. In either case, frontier emerging markets must be assessed in light of the dimension of market segmentation theory. Without it, any exercise would neglect one of the most fundamental and powerful forces underlying securities price behavior in frontier emerging markets.

Appendix I to chapter V.

Table 5.1. Cumulative brokerage report coverage

	GAZP	NZGZ	NYGS	MFGS	ORNB	TOMG	LKOH	CHGZ	YFGA	SNGS	PFGS	UES	LEN	MSNG	IRGZ	MGTS	SPTL	RTKM	GUMM	KMAZ	GAZA	FESH	NKEL
95/1	0	0	0	0	0	0	0	0	0	0	0	0	0	0	0	0	0	0	0	0	0	0	0
95/2	1	1	1	1	0	1	2	1	0	1	1	2	0	0	0	1	2	2	0	0	0	0	2
95/3	1	2	2	2	1	2	3	2	1	2	2	2	0	0	0	1	2	2	0	0	0	0	2
95/4	2	3	3	3	2	3	5	3	2	3	3	3	1	1	1	2	3	3	0	1	1	1	3
95/5	2	3	4	4	2	3	6	3	2	4	3	3	1	1	1	2	3	3	0	1	1	1	3
95/6	2	3	4	4	2	3	7	4	2	5	3	3	1	1	2	3	4	5	0	1	1	1	3
95/7	2	3	4	4	2	3	7	4	2	5	3	3	1	1	2	3	4	5	0	1	1	2	3
95/8	2	3	4	4	2	3	7	4	2	5	3	3	1	1	2	4	5	6	0	1	1	2	3
95/9	2	3	4	4	2	3	8	4	2	5	3	3	1	3	2	4	5	7	0	1	1	2	3
95/10	2	3	4	4	2	3	8	4	2	5	3	4	1	3	2	4	5	7	0	1	1	2	3
95/11	2	3	4	4	2	3	8	4	2	5	3	4	1	3	2	4	5	7	0	1	1	2	3
95/12	2	3	4	4	2	3	8	4	2	5	3	4	1	3	2	4	5	7	0	1	1	2	3
96/1	2	3	4	4	2	3	9	4	2	5	3	4	1	4	2	4	5	7	0	1	1	2	3
96/2	2	3	4	4	2	3	10	4	2	5	3	4	1	4	2	4	5	8	0	1	1	2	3
96/3	2	4	5	5	3	4	13	6	2	7	4	4	1	5	2	4	5	8	0	2	1	2	4
96/4	2	4	6	7	3	4	15	6	2	8	4	5	2	6	4	4	5	8	1	2	2	3	5
96/5	3	5	7	8	4	5	15	7	2	9	5	8	3	9	7	4	5	8	1	2	3	3	5
96/6	4	6	8	9	5	6	17	10	4	11	6	9	3	11	7	6	7	10	1	3	3	4	5
96/7	5	6	9	11	5	7	19	11	4	12	6	9	3	12	7	7	7	11	2	3	3	5	5
96/8	6	6	9	11	5	7	20	11	4	12	6	9	3	15	7	7	7	12	5	4	4	5	5
96/9	9	6	10	11	6	7	25	12	4	13	6	10	3	16	7	8	8	14	7	4	4	6	5
96/10	12	6	10	11	6	7	25	13	5	14	6	10	3	18	7	8	10	18	8	5	4	7	5
96/11	12	9	10	12	7	8	27	18	7	15	7	10	4	19	9	8	11	19	9	5	4	7	5
96/12	13	9	10	12	8	8	29	19	7	15	8	13	6	22	11	9	13	23	9	5	4	7	7
97/1	13	9	10	13	9	8	31	20	8	18	8	13	6	23	11	10	15	27	11	5	4	7	8
97/2	13	9	10	13	9	8	32	22	8	20	8	13	6	24	13	12	16	28	12	5	4	7	8
97/3	13	10	10	13	9	8	34	21	8	21	8	16	7	26	15	12	16	30	14	5	5	7	8
97/4	16	10	10	13	9	8	35	21	8	21	8	17	7	27	15	12	16	30	14	6	6	7	8
97/5	17	10	10	13	9	8	35	21	8	22	8	18	7	27	15	14	17	32	16	6	6	8	8
97/6	18	11	10	15	10	10	37	21	9	24	8	18	7	30	15	14	18	32	16	6	7	8	8
97/7	19	11	10	15	10	10	38	21	9	24	8	18	8	31	15	16	20	34	16	7	7	8	8
97/8	19	11	11	16	10	10	38	21	9	24	8	21	8	33	15	17	20	35	16	8	8	8	10
97/9	21	11	11	16	10	10	39	21	9	24	8	22	8	34	17	17	20	36	16	8	9	8	10

Chapter 6

Econometrics of Measuring Frontier Equity Market Efficiency
Quantitative insights into unquantifiable areas

There are two main purposes for conducting tests of market efficiency in frontier emerging equity markets: (1) to detect allocational inefficiencies in the market, and (2) to detect unexploited profit opportunities, which imply informational inefficiency. The first purpose can be viewed in a larger economic context, where allocational efficiency implies that capital resources are channeled to those firms which are most deserving of investment. Those companies are projected to create an economic benefit to society as a whole by developing products or services that enjoy sufficient demand and that succeed in generating at least the minimum required rate of return for the companies' shareholders.

The second purpose, in reality, is simply a derivative of the first one. If market inefficiency is discovered by market participants, the first motion would be to exploit it until it ceased to exist. Strictly speaking, the sheer existence of informational market inefficiency implies that allocational inefficiency must have been in place as well, as the schedule of securities' price behavior, which theoretically should be dictated by fundamentals and all other information relevant to the asset, had not been reflected in the share price as quickly and accurately as market efficiency would demand. Therefore any profit opportunity based on informational market inefficiency results from a lack of true representation of the fair demand schedule for an asset as it would be dictated by its characteristics.

The measurement of market efficiency has been a problem which financial economists have debated now for almost 100 years (given Bachelier's 1900 exploratory thesis on the subject). Yet there has been little consensus so far.   As already pointed out in the chapter 2, there is an increasing number of tests that fill an exploding number of pages in journals dedicated to financial economics. However, as Eugene Fama, the pioneer of the efficient market hypothesis, stated in one of his early essays:

"In an uncertain world, no amount of empirical testing is sufficient to establish the validity [of the random walk hypothesis or any alternative hypothesis] beyond any shadow of doubt."[1]

In this book, and specifically for the reasons mentioned above, the random walk model serves well to measure relative market efficiency as it captures the two dimensions of allocational market efficiency, and informational market efficiency.[2] While there is a growing number of new approaches dedicated to describing securities price behavior, ranging from models with time-varying parameters (such as models with GARCH [Generalized Autoregressive Conditionally Heteroscedasticity] components) to models based on neural networks, the variance ratio test of the random walk model seems the most intuitive.   Even though subject to some criticism, the variance ratio test is a fairly robust model which has been broadly defended in academic research dedicated to securities price behavior.[3]   Furthermore, its robustness to many forms of non-normality and heteroscedasticity in the data qualify the variance ratio test for the special case of non-normally distributed, and possibly heteroscedasticity-exhibiting returns of frontier market equities.

If a new model were found to fully describe the process of securities price behavior, a case could be made for adopting such methodology over variance ratio or other random walk-based approaches. The creator of such a model, however, would do well by not publishing it, but instead by applying it to proprietary trading and reaping its rewards. Therefore, for the time being, for the non-measurability of a possible superiority of alternative models, and, above all, for the primary purpose of measuring relative as opposed to absolute market efficiency, tests of the random walk model, and

---

[1] Eugene F. Fama, "Random Walks in Stock Prices," *Financial Analysts Journal* (September/October 1965): 55-59.
[2] In this dual-purpose context, the random walk model is superior to cointegration-based tests which primarily focus on the relationship of two or more assets, and thus allow for drawing conclusions on the predictability of at least one of them.
[3] The variance ratio test will be described in detail in a later section in the chapter.

specifically via the conduit of variance ratio tests, serve well to describe relative market efficiency.

VI.A.   From random walk to relative market efficiency

VI.A.1.   The random walk model as a tool to measure market efficiency

The connection between the efficient market hypothesis (EMH) and the random walk as a measurement tool has been elaborately established by many researchers over time.[4] The following paragraphs serve to recapitulate the most important technical assumptions underlying the random walk model as a tool for measuring relative market efficiency.

One of the fundamental premises of EMH is that the price of an actively traded asset reflects an optimal use of all available information. This general condition can be illustrated by assuming that the market participant can think of each sequence of events affecting the asset as a 'state-of-the-world.' The number of different 'states-of-the-world' is infinite [state-of-the-world $s=(1,2,3,...,N)$]. Further, suppose that the aggregated set of all information available at time t is denoted by Ω_t and that $\pi(s\,|\,\Omega_t)$ is the probability that state s will occur, conditional on the total information available at time t. Based on this premise, or each state-of-the-world, a fundamental value of the asset can be derived, which can be denoted as $P^*(s)$. Accordingly, there are N fundamental values. If P_t is the current market price and the *expected* fundamental value is $E(P_t^*\,|\,\Omega_t)=\Sigma_s\ P^*(s)\ \pi(s\,|\,\Omega_t)$, then the EMH is embodied in the equation,

$$P_t = E(P_t^*\,|\,\Omega_t) \tag{1}$$

which states that the current price of an asset is the best estimate of its fundamental value.

---

[4] For a recent, and enlightening discussion on the random walk see: Peter Fortune, "Stock Market Efficiency: An Autopsy?" *The New England Economic Review* (March/April 1991): 19-20.

Box 6.0. Illustration of derivation of best estimate of fundamental value

---

Illustration of derivation of expected fundamental value

Consider the example below: There are three possible outcomes to the initial situation described in the first box. Each outcome (or state-of-the-world s) is associated with a probability. The probability of outcomes s would be $\pi(s \mid \Omega_t)$. Then the expected fundamental value can be simplistically derived as outlined below:

Dec. 12, 1997

Russian President Boris Yeltsin withdraws from Kremlin and checks into sanatorium outside of Moscow. Officially he suffers from a cold. The market needs to form its own opinion...

| π 70% | π 20% | π 10% |

State of the world

| Yeltsin recovers fully | Yeltsin does not recover and loses his mind as already had been indicated during his visit in Sweden, when he referred to Germany and Japan as nuclear powers... | Yeltsin dies |

| Yeltsin returns | Yeltsin's daughter, Boris Berezovsky and Chubais form a caretaker government until early elections are called in 3 months |

| Tatneft is fairly valued at $140 | The price of Tatneft drops to $80 as political risk premium increases and production-sharing agreements are under threat... |

$$E(P_t^* \mid \Omega_t)$$

Price $= 30\% * \$80 + 70\% * \$140 = \$122$

Another strong implication of the EMH can be derived from the fact that Ω_t contains all relevant information at time t. Accordingly, the unanticipated component of the market price would be uncorrelated with any relevant information available at time t, which includes past price behavior, current fundamental data and all future projections relevant to the security, industry, or market. A test of this proposition would be to run a regression of P_t on a measure of the optimal forecast $E(P_t^* | \Omega_t)$ and also on any information that might be in Ω_t (for example the history of stock prices or any other historical information on the stock). The result should indicate a correlation coefficient of 1 for $E(P_t^* | \Omega_t)$ and a correlation coefficient of 0 for Ω_t which then would suggest that all information (such as historical stock prices) has been embedded in the fundamental value.

The second implication of the EMH describes the price development sequence over time. In order to forecast the asset price at time t+1, the forecast would be ideally derived from $E(P_{t+1}^* | \Omega_{t+1})$. Given, however, that at time t, the information available at t+1 is not known, the information contained in Ω_t is all the information available to forecast the price at time t. Hence, the best forecast would be $E(P_{t+1}^* | \Omega_t)$. Furthermore, the investor may know the required rate of return of the asset, which can be denoted as r.[5] From this logic and equation (1), the optimal forecast definition, the EMH implies the following sequence of price development:

$$P_{t+1} = (1+r)P_t + \varepsilon_{t+1}, \text{ where } E(\varepsilon_{t+1}) = 0 \qquad (2)$$

From equation (2) one can derive that any new information between time t and t+1 is random, thus, by definition, the change between P_{t+1} and the best forecast is random.[6] Following from this, equation (2) describes a random walk with drift where prices will vary randomly around a rising trend. This is the basis for using the random walk as a tool to test for EMH by examining price series for correlated increments.

VI.A.2. Practical implications of deviation from the random walk

On a more practical note the concept of predictable markets would imply that investors who are aware of it can profit at the expense of those who are

---

[5] In this demonstration the dividend is ignored as it contains little relevance for the Russian market or any other pre-emerging market. The required rate of return is also highly dynamic in the Russian context and the same logical steps could be applied to it as have been applied to the price formation mechanism.

[6] ε_{t+1} has a zero mean and no serial correlation.

not.[7] Then it may be just a matter of time until less 'informed' investors no longer participate in such a market, thus reducing the liquidity, resilience and depth of the market. In a mature market, investors may not give up so easily as they would possibly try to become 'informed' investors and work towards positioning themselves on the other side of the uneven playing field. In pre-emerging markets, where insider trading and corporate decisions are often exclusively shared among the country's political and business elites before foreigners are informed, the likelihood of foreigners withdrawing investments because they cannot realistically assume to become part of the 'information elite' in a pre-emerging market, is considerably higher. Therefore, pre-emerging markets cannot afford gross departures from random walk behavior and price non-predictability, if its policy makers seriously intend to position their market on the map of global finance and investment.

The alternative is to remain a predictable securities market which enhances the wealth of the local informed insiders at the cost of a few 'cowboy closed-end funds' which, by mandate, remain dedicated to the market, regardless of the uneven playing field.

VI.B. Three types of random walks and the variance ratio test

VI.B.1. Random walk 1 (RW1), RW2, and RW3

As already outlined in chapter 2, there are three types of random walks.[8] The explanation for choosing RW3 given in chapter 2 will be reiterated at this point for reasons of comprehension.

Campbell, Lo and MacKinlay define three types of the random walk (RW): RW1 assumes identically and independently distributed increments (IID), RW2 assumes independently and not identically distributed increments (INID), and RW3 assumes uncorrelated increments. RW1 can be

---

[7] In this context, Fama notes that weak-form market efficiency can be rejected if past behavior in a securities price series reveals patterns that can be identified and turned into a profit through the application of a pattern-exploiting trading strategy.

[8] Please refer to the following literature for a detailed description of the three types of random walk hypotheses, (RW1, RW2, and RW3): John Y. Campbell, Andrew W. Lo, and A. Craig MacKinlay, *Econometrics of Financial Markets* (Princeton, N.J. Princeton University Press: 1997): 28-33.

tested with sequences and reversals, and runs tests. RW2 can be tested with filter rules. RW3, the random walk assumption used in this study, can be tested with autocorrelation tests and variance ratio tests. The notion of the three different random walk assumptions carries a particular weight in the context of emerging markets. There are at least two reasons why the assumption of RW3 in emerging markets appears more optimal than RW1 or RW2: Firstly, RWI assumes IID and RW2 assumes INID. Both assumptions are relatively less representative of emerging markets price behavior where heteroscedasticity and non-normality can be common characteristics. Although RW2 allows for unconditional heteroscedasticty, RW3 remains a safer assumption over RW2 since it does allow some transformation of future price increments to be forecastable using some transformation of past price increments. This RW3 assumption can be defined as:

$$\text{Cov}[\varepsilon_t, \varepsilon_{t-k}] = 0 \text{ for all } k \neq 0 \text{, but where } \text{Cov}[\varepsilon_t^2, \varepsilon_{t-k}^2] \neq 0 \text{ for some } k \neq 0$$

As opposed to RW1 or RW2, this process has uncorrelated increments but is not independent since its squared increments are correlated in some cases.

Secondly, RW2-based methodologies, such as filter rules or trading rules seem less optimal in the pre-emerging market environment where paper trading simulations (or filter rules based on trading simulations) are difficult, if not impossible, to conduct given the often opaque trading environment where bid/ask quotes may not reflect the real execution price at all times, and transaction costs may vary considerably, and thus would render a simulation-based test practically meaningless.

VI.B.2.   Test of the Random walk 3 (RW3) with the variance ratio test

To test for the random walk, the variance ratio test proposed by Lo and MacKinlay (1988) is applied.[9] The methodology follows Lo and MacKinlay (1988) conceptually, and Liu and He (1991) in its mechanical application

---

[9] John Y. Campbell, Andrew W. Lo, and A. Craig MacKinlay, *Econometrics of Financial Markets* (Princeton, N.J. Princeton University Press: 1997): 66-74.

A.W. Lo and A MacKinlay, "Stock Market Prices Do Not Follow Random Walks: Evidence from a Simple Specification Test," *The Review of Financial Studies*, vol 1, no 1 (1988):41-66.

for testing the random walk. Hence, it is based on Liu and He's focus on the uncorrelated increments aspect.[10] As other variance ratio tests, Lo and MacKinlay's variance ratio test exploits the fact that the variance of the increments in a random walk is linear in the sampling interval. This implies that the natural logarithm of a price series can be described by the random walk process, if the variance of its q-differences is q times the variance of its first differences. For example, the variance measured over weekly intervals would be ¼ of the variance measured over monthly intervals. Therefore, with $nq+1$ stock price observations S_0, S_1, S_2,...., S_{nq} at equally spaced intervals (q is an integer greater than one), the ratio of $1/q$ of the variance $S_t - S_{t-q}$ to the variance of $S_t - S_{t-1}$ would be equal to one.[11]

As Liu and He (1991) point out, the variance ratio test is unique for the following reasons. A standard normal test statistic for the variance ratio is derived by first forming an asymptotic distribution of the variance ratio.[12] The Z-statistic is then calculated by comparing the sample variance ratio with the asymptotic variance of the variance ratio. Furthermore, a refined, heteroscedasticity-consistent, Z^*-statistic is developed.

The heteroscedasticity-consistent test statistic meets a growing consensus among financial economists that financial time series are often not normally distributed and that volatility changes over time. For that reason, a simple rejection of the random walk model due to heteroscedasticity would be of little interest. In addition, the deviation from normality observed in Russian and other frontier market equity returns requires a test that is robust to many forms of non-normality. The variance ratio test of RW3 meets this requirement.

MacKinlay and Lo (1989) prove with a Monte Carlo experiment that under a heteroscedasticity random walk, the variance ratio test is more reliable than the Box-Pierce Q-test.[13] Furthermore, the variance ratio test is as or more powerful than the Box-Pierce or Dickey Fuller test against

[10] Liu and He acknowledge that the random walk has two implications: the unit root and uncorrelated increments. The focus on uncorrelated increments is based on the notion that there are some important departures from the random walk that unit root tests cannot detect - refer to Liu and He (1991).

[11] Strictly speaking, the condition of equally spaced intervals cannot be met in the test on hand as consecutive trading days are observed as opposed to consecutive calendar days.

[12] Christina Y. Liu and Jia He, "A Variance Ratio Test of the Random Walks in Foreign Exchange Rates," *Journal of Finance*, vol 46, no 2 (June 1991): 773-785.

[13] Andrew W. Lo and Craig MacKinlay, "The Size and Power of the Variance Ratio Test in Finite Samples: A Monte Carlo Investigation," *Journal of Econometrics*, 40 (1989): 203-238.

various alternative hypotheses, including an AR(1), an ARIMA(1,1,1), and an ARIMA(1,1,0).

VI.B.3. Computation of the variance ratio test

Henceforth the calculation of the variance ratio, and the variance ratio test statistics are presented. The variance ratio, VR(q):

(3)

$$VR(q) = \frac{\sigma_c^2(q)}{\sigma_a^2(q)},$$

Variance of first differences of a log time series

where $\sigma_c^2(q)$ is an unbiased estimator of $1/q$ of the variance of the qth difference of the natural log of the price series S_t, and $\sigma_a^2(q)$ is an unbiased estimator of the variance of the first difference of S_t. The formulas for calculating $\sigma_c^2(q)$ and $\sigma_a^2(q)$ are given below in equations (4) and (5):

(4)

$$\sigma_c^2(q) = \frac{1}{m} \sum_{t=q}^{nq} (S_t - S_{t-q} - q\hat{\mu})^2,$$

with μ defined as

$$\hat{\mu} = \frac{1}{nq}(S_{nq} - S_0)$$

where $m = (nq-q+1)(1-q/nq)$, and where

(5)

$$\sigma_a^2(q) = \frac{1}{nq-1}\sum_{t=1}^{nq}(S_t - S_{t-1} - \hat{\mu})^2,$$

The asymptotic variance of the variance-ratio under homoscedasticity, $\phi(q)$, is then:

(6)

$$\phi(q) = \frac{2(2q-1)(q-1)}{3q(nq)}$$

The standard normal test statistic under homoscedasticity, $Z(q)$, is then:

(7)

$$Z(q) = \frac{VR(q)-1}{[\phi(q)]^{\frac{1}{2}}} \approx N(0,1)$$

The heteroscedasticity-consistent asymptotic variance of the variance-ratio, $\phi^*(q)$:

(8)

$$\phi^*(q) = \sum_{j=1}^{q-1}\left[\frac{2(q-j)}{q}\right]^2 \hat{\delta}(j)$$

where

(9)

$$\hat{\delta}(j) = \frac{\sum\limits_{t=j+1}^{nq}(S_t - S_{t-1} - \hat{\mu})^2(S_{t-j} - S_{t-j-1} - \hat{\mu})^2}{\left[\sum\limits_{k=1}^{nq}(S_t - S_{t-1} - \hat{\mu})^2\right]^2}$$

The heteroscedasticity-consistent standard normal test-statistic, $Z^*(q)$ then follows below:

(10)

$$Z^*(q) = \frac{VR(q) - 1}{\left[\phi^*(q)\right]^{1/2}} \approx N(0,1)$$

The first-order autocorrelation coefficient can be approximately estimated from the following equations. The population properties of variance ratios are described by Campbell, Lo and MacKinlay (1997) as follows:

(11)

$$r_t(2) \equiv r_t + r_{t-1} \text{ (a two-period return)}$$

$$r_t \quad \text{(a one-period return)}$$

> This describes the variance of a two-period return divided by two times the variance of a one period return.

$$VR(2) = \frac{Var[r_t(2)]}{2Var[r_t]} = \frac{Var[r_t + r_{t-1}]}{2Var[r_t]} = \frac{2Var[r_t] + 2Cov[r_t, r_{t-1}]}{2Var[r_r]}$$

which can be re-written as

$$VR(2) = 1 + 2\rho(1)$$

where $\rho(1)$ is the first-order autocorrelation coefficient for returns r_t.

Specifically, the tests are conducted by analyzing the full time period for all securities for which sufficient data is available, which accounts for 660 observations per security. Additionally, in order to capture the changing degree of support or rejection of the random walk over time, nine equally spaced intervals, each comprising 73 observations are analyzed with the same tests.[14]

For previous applications of the variance ratio test, the reader may refer to studies on the Korean securities market, various Latin American equity markets, a sample of the IFC emerging equity markets universe, as well as to random walk studies on the US equity market, and several pairs of G-7 exchange rates.[15]

---

[14] Based on Monte Carlo experiments performed by Lo and MacKinlay (1989), the empirical two-sided five percent variance-ratio tests are close to their nominal values for sample sizes greater than 32. As Liu and He (1991) point out, the conclusion has been obtained in their work under the null hypothesis of random walks, with either homoscedastic or heteroscedastic disturbances. Since the sample size for the subperiods is 73, the adoption of the Z- and Z* -statistic seems justifiable.

[15] Ayadi and Pyun (1994); Urrutia (1995); Claessens, Dasgupta and Glen (1993); Campbell, MacKinlay and Lo (1997); Liu and He (1991).

VI.C. The variance test applied to the pre-emerging equity market of Russia

It must be noted that the rejection of the random walk model may not necessarily imply inefficiency of the Russian equity market, or that prices are not derived from rational assessments of all the news available. The implications of a rejection of the random walk are not to disprove market efficiency – although some equilibrium pricing models can be rejected – but to show the changing nature of the relative strength of the random walk model for individual and groups of Russian securities. From this follows that relative market inefficiency cannot necessarily be translated into trading gains. It is, however, applicable to a comparative analysis of securities, or of portfolios with specific characteristics, which display relative signs of market efficiency and inefficiency vis-à-vis each other. The comparative analysis resulting from such testing methodology is significant, for it will be those results which can create a blue-print for changing characteristics which can be related to securities that exhibit a lower degree of relative market efficiency.

In defense of the notion of *relative* market efficiency it can be claimed that tests of absolute market efficiency are an indication of idealism in purpose but failed realism in method. A measure of absolute market efficiency, which would *optimally* capture the price behavior process is unlikely to exist. Methods including time-varying parameters, such as changing volatility, changing risk premia or adding Bayesian components and neural networks to the model, should be applied to investing money in a profit-seeking way. This would be more meaningful, if any value could be derived from such a model, other than filling pages in academic journals.[16] This, along with the harsh reality that price behavior cannot be captured simply by econometric models, probably serves as the strongest argument for the measurement of relative market efficiency as opposed to absolute market efficiency.

In addition, the concept of market efficiency takes on a new meaning in a frontier equity market such as Russia, where the premises of the EMH, as

---

[16] Indeed, this would add more value, as those market inefficiencies that have been discovered could at least be eliminated via some type of arbitrage based on a superior model. Most of the time, new 'sophisticated' theory in this field does not venture beyond the academic journals, and therefore fails to add value to the functioning of financial markets, and society as a whole.

outlined in chapter 2, partially do not hold.[17] Therefore, strict adherence to any absolute measure of EMH derived from the five assumptions, would logically be destined to fail and hence be a misdirected attempt on the subject, particular with reference to a frontier equity market.

---

[17] The assumption of a large number of rational and profit-maximizing investors is violated. Prices are often a function of accumulating ownership share, as opposed to seeking profit. Price-taking behavior is questionable, as the analogy of the roach motel frequently holds: "You can buy shares but you cannot sell them without problems as the frontier market brokers' quote will fall on the indication of a sell intention."

Chapter 7

Running the Numbers on a Frontier Market
Of noise and stealth traders

In Chapter 5, the discussion was concluded by creating three different portfolios for the Russian equity market according to individual securities' transparency: the top-, medium-, and bottom-transparency portfolio. For the purpose of measuring relative market efficiency, this chapter will use these three portfolios and apply to them the variance ratio test discussed in chapter 6.

In the second section of this chapter, evolving relative market efficiency will be examined by applying the variance ratio test to the Russian market index between January 1995 and September 1997.

VII.A. Relative market efficiency and security transparency

VII.A.1. Presentation of results

The plausible notion that higher transparency and a higher degree of information release about a company translate into higher informational efficiency and thus a higher degree of relative market efficiency, as market participants will be able to react more quickly and accurately to news information on their stocks, has been the subject of this test. The results of table 7.0., which presents the homoscedasticity-and heteroscedasticity-robust test scores of the variance ratio test, show that the top-transparency portfolio defeats the random walk in 100% of all cases, the bottom-transparency portfolio defeats the random walk in 80% of all cases, and the medium-transparency portfolio defeats the random walk in only 46% of all cases.[1] Diagram 7.0. illustrates these findings.

These results suggest that mechanisms are at work in the highly-transparent blue-chip stocks, which translate into the same effect as the one we observe in the low-transparency portfolio, where the returns process can be described in a more predictable, less random fashion than in the medium-transparency portfolio. It also implies that the effects of higher transparency are possibly outweighed by another factor which comes into play. This other factor is market segmentation, which will be discussed in section VII.A.2.

Diagram 7.0. Relative market efficiency and securities transparency

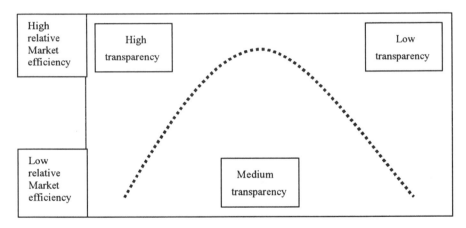

The rationale why the low-transparency portfolio defeats the random walk is easily explained by the commonly accepted notion that a lack of information does not allow investors to quickly and accurately act upon fundamental news of the company. In such a situation, investors learn about news gradually and the returns process is described by autocorrelated increments.

The medium-transparency portfolio, which to a larger degree can be described by a random walk, even under the assumption of heteroscedasticity in the data, is better researched and enjoys better information dissemination than the low-transparency portfolio. Thus the closer adherence to the random walk process seems plausible, as investors can react more quickly and accurately to new information.

---

[1] The more conservative heteroscedasticity-robust z*-scores are used.

The initially counterintuitive findings about the top-transparency portfolio, leaves some room for speculation at first. However, when considering the unique environment of a frontier equity market and its foreign participants, reason can be prudently applied and a plausible explanation can be formulated.

VII.A.2. Relative market inefficiency - a case of market segmentation

Samuelson cites substantial evidence that prices are most likely predictable under circumstances when there are no high-powered 'analyst whizzes' following a company, or only a few, than when there are many.[2] This view is based on the fact that well-informed analysts will react to news about a security more cohesively and instantaneously than a group of 'low-powered' analysts. The less dedicated analysts are more likely to pick up the relevant news pieces gradually and consequently act upon the news information less instantaneously, thus introducing autocorrelation to price returns series.

This leads to the first argument which creates a reasonable basis for understanding the defiance of the random walk when examining Russian blue-chips that benefit from transparency, liquidity and investment channels unparalleled in the lower transparency portfolios. While the high powered 'analyst whizzes' of the medium-sized portfolio are to some degree involved in stocks composing the top-transparency portfolio, (a) they count less in number than in the medium-sized portfolio, and (b) they are overshadowed by trading volume of 'low-powered' general international equity analysts.[3]

Investing in Russia has become more than a passing fancy, and an increasing number of foreign investors, tempted by the worlds largest returns during the initial phase between 1995 and mid-1997, had entered the market. An increasing number of their less astute brethren - mainly non-dedicated international mutual funds - followed in their footsteps, often as a result of peer performance pressure. This frequently was the very first time main stream investment funds, managing substantial amounts of assets, gained exposure to Russia. For those participants, an average position had to amount to between $4-$15 million, in order for it to be significant in an average-sized non-emerging market-dedicated international equity portfolio.

---

[2] Peter L. Bernstein, *Capital Ideas,* (New York: The Free Press, 1993): 123.

[3] Dedicated Russia analysts often refer to the stocks in the top-transparency portfolio as 'no-brainers' indicating that less time is spent on their analysis than on medium-transparency stocks. Further, the law of the marginal bidder setting the price does not hold in this situation due to segmented on-shore and off-shore trading activity which implies that foreigners are trading among each other in large volumes via Western brokers (market makers in the stock), and small dedicated funds are trading among each other.

However, in building their positions, liquidity was required. The only stocks that offered such liquidity throughout the time span examined, were the top-transparency blue chips. Furthermore, Russia-inexperienced sector buy-side analysts needed research so they had some basic reason to justify their decision during investment decision meetings. The stocks which offered the most reliable continuous coverage were in the top-transparency portfolio. This finally led to a swamping effect in the top-transparency portfolio, where relatively unsophisticated investors, in the context of frontier market equities, outnumbered the few Russia-dedicated pioneers.[4] This interpretation has also been adopted by the IMF, which observed positive autocorrelation as a result of uninformed foreign institutional investors.[5]

The most comprehensive explanation of this phenomenon, however, is presented by adherents of a theory which has become known as 'noise trading'. Noise trading falls in the general framework of market segmentation theory. A simple model of noise trading was presented by DeLong, Shleifer, Summers and Waldmann (1990).[6] This model assumes that sophisticated investors (dedicated emerging market funds in our case) form optimal forecasts of the future price, and unsophisticated investors (generally non-frontier market-dedicated international equity funds in our case), also called 'noise traders', form biased forecasts. The question of why sophisticated investors do not dominate the market by forcing the market price to equal its fundamental value via arbitrage, is a function of the risk aversion of sophisticated investors. According to the 'noise trader model', sophisticated investors are risk averse. A potential arbitrage is considered too risky as sophisticated investors are never sure as to when and in what direction noise traders' price misperceptions change. Thus, the impact of noise traders can never be fully arbitraged away.[7]

---

[4] On the subject of unsophisticated market participants: Fischer Black, "Noise," *The Journal of Finance*, vol 41, no 3 (1986): 529-543.

[5] Anthony J. Richards, "Volatility and Predictability in National Stock Markets, " *IMF Staff Papers*, vol 43, no 3 (September 1996): 461-501.

[6] Delong, J. Bradford; Andrei Shleifer; Lawrence H. Summers and Robert J. Waldmann. "Noise Trader Risk in Financial Markets." *Journal of Political Economy* (August 1990): 703-738.

[7] The explanation of why sophisticated investors are not setting the price via arbitrage (as a result of risk-aversion and the awareness that noise traders can change their perception based on information not related to the fundamentals of the underlying investments), can be well applied to the 1998/99 internet stock euphoria where unsophisticated day traders control substantial amounts of the free float of the so-called "dot.coms."

Relative market inefficiencies therefore become predominant in those securities which are dominated by a larger percentage of unsophisticated investors, or noise traders. This model, applied to the above referred 'swamping' effect of dedicated Russia analysts by non-dedicated general international equity analysts in the top-transparency portfolio, explains the lower degree of relative market efficiency in the top-transparency portfolio. This effect did not take place in the medium-transparency portfolio, which remains dominated by smaller, more dedicated emerging markets investors, who are less constrained by their compliance departments to invest freely in Russian equities. Compliance departments, affecting large non-specialized international mutual funds, play another role in building the rationale for the effect we are observing. Once compliance departments have conceded to investing in a frontier market, mutual fund managers are not likely to become 'flippers' in a market that is not within their investment mandate in the first place.[8] Hence, a larger number of buy-and-hold strategies prevails than rational expectations theory would allow in the context of market efficiency. Lastly, non-dedicated foreign investors also incur higher transaction costs than their local Moscow-based counterparts. Although brokers mostly quote net prices, international investors pay the premium created by Western brokerages' profit margins in addition to the local brokerages' profit margins. This higher transaction costs-based situation, is another argument supporting a buy-and-hold strategy, rather than an investment strategy which would allow for action whenever new information enters the market.[9]

Finally, to recapitulate, there are three main reasons why the efficient market hypothesis is violated in the top transparency portfolio: (1) securities trading in this portfolio are dominated by less dedicated investors who are acting less quickly and accurately upon new information because a frontier market is only a marginal concern in their portfolio and they lack the resources to have staff fully committed to feeling the pulse of the market on a daily basis, (2) a large number of noise traders is present in the top-transparency portfolio, and (3) less dedicated investors are acting less quickly and less accurately because of institutional-, infrastructure-, and transaction cost-based reasons.[10] All arguments support the finding that the

---

[8] "Flippers" refer to investors that buy securities and sell them quickly thereafter, often in connection with IPOs.

[9] A buy-and-hold behavior does not necessarily lead to autocorrelated prices, but it does if foreigners, which is the case in Russia, often unload securities in herd-like fashions once the top-down outlook of a pre-emerging market changes.

[10] In the context of noise traders' vs smart money's impact on financial markets also refer to: Morgan Kelly, "Do Noise Traders Influence Stock Prices," *Money, Credit and Banking* (1991): 351-363.

top-transparency portfolio displays more signs of defiance of the random walk than the medium-transparency portfolio. This discussion is graphically displayed in diagram 7.1.

Diagram 7.1.   Market segmentation causes different degrees of relative market efficiency

Investor type	Cause for segmentation	Portfolio transparency	Causes for different degrees of relative market efficiency
Non-dedicated general international equity investor	Need liquidity Need research Need compliance approval	Top-transparency portfolio	1. Noise trader model 2. Less informed, react more slowly to new information ⇒autocorrelated increments 3. Higher transaction costs ⇒ more sticky prices 4. Cannot become flippers as easily – even if required by information 5. Stealth trading applies
Dedicated-pre-emerging market investor	Less compliance restrictions Dedicated to conduct own research No liquidity restrictions	Medium-transparency portfolio	1. Astute followers of new information ⇒ 'instantaneous' trading reaction 2. Flippers if necessary 3. No stealth trading required due to smaller positions 4. Lower transaction costs, if located in Russia – also trading with low-cost brokers since brokerage research is largely irrelevant

Table 7.0. Heteroscedasticity/homoscedasticity-consistent variance-ratio test statistics

	full period	95-1-10/95-4-20	95-4-21/95-8-11	95-8-14/95-11-22	95-11-23/96-3-14	96-3-15/96-6-20	96-7-1/96-10-1	96-10-10/97-1-24	97-1-27/97-5-13	97-5-14/97-8-27
SNGS										
z^*	3.90	0.69	3.24	-1.10	-0.03	2.60	1.63	0.62	2.63	0.23
z	6.38	0.76	3.27	-1.16	-0.04	2.71	1.94	0.74	3.12	0.36
PFGS										
z^*	3.11	1.05	3.16	1.89	0.11	0.33	1.95	2.05	1.02	-0.36
z	4.21	1.30	3.27	2.00	0.13	0.39	2.29	2.33	1.22	-0.51
VFGA										
z^*	4.73	4.71	2.38	1.97	-0.99	2.06	1.66	-0.09	0.13	1.04
z	6.45	5.49	2.46	2.09	-1.23	2.41	1.87	-0.11	0.16	1.50
MFGS										
z^*	3.11	2.83	0.74	-0.64	-0.52	0.29	2.05	2.36	0.56	0.32
z	4.21	3.38	0.80	-0.67	-0.64	0.32	2.44	2.80	0.67	0.49
NYGS										
z^*	2.67	2.52	2.10	-1.10	1.69	1.68	1.13	0.57	2.50	-0.50
z	3.63	2.89	2.11	-1.17	2.11	1.96	1.32	0.67	2.98	-0.80
TOMG										
z^*	1.71	2.08	1.72	0.28	0.09	0.70	0.95	0.66	0.41	-1.05
z	2.32	2.33	1.76	0.30	0.11	0.80	1.09	0.80	0.49	-1.54
NZGZ										
z^*	1.15	1.02	-1.89	-0.74	1.37	0.34	0.58	-0.33	0.05	1.76
z	1.57	1.25	-1.82	-0.78	-1.71	0.41	0.69	-0.41	0.06	2.07
CHGZ										
z^*	0.70	-3.18	-0.20	0.94	-0.36	1.78	-0.14	-0.59	-0.57	1.08
z	0.95	-4.05	-0.21	0.99	-0.45	2.12	-0.16	-0.70	-0.69	1.65
ORNB										
z^*	-0.81	-0.78	-0.68	0.90	1.55	-1.65	-0.17	0.42	2.10	-0.63
z	-1.09	-0.97	-0.70	0.94	1.93	-1.83	-0.20	0.47	2.48	-1.00
GAZP										
z^*	-1.42	-1.97	-0.43	-2.00	-1.93	4.40	0.53	-0.01	1.26	3.16
z	-1.91	-2.45	-0.46	-2.11	-2.41	5.27	0.69	-0.01	1.50	4.85
RTKM										
z^*	2.50	2.97	1.46	0.95	0.23	-0.07	1.49	1.08	1.53	1.13
z	3.47	3.78	1.51	1.01	0.27	-0.07	1.82	1.34	1.83	1.79
SPTL										
z^*	2.83	0.87	-0.57	0.74	1.89	1.09	1.07	3.59	0.85	2.74
z	3.83	1.09	-0.61	0.78	-2.36	1.27	2.34	4.03	1.02	4.19
MGTS										
z^*	2.31	-1.92	-1.08	-0.74	-1.01	-0.02	1.95	2.82	2.89	2.09
z	3.08	-2.45	-1.16	-0.78	-1.23	-0.03	2.47	3.36	3.41	3.08
GUMM										
z^*	-0.13	-0.65	-0.64	-2.26	-1.03	3.59	1.57	1.69	1.72	0.03
z	-0.17	-0.82	-0.70	-2.37	-1.27	4.09	1.92	1.98	2.06	0.04
NKEL										
z^*	2.26	0.60	1.03	0.47	-0.32	1.35	2.51	1.55	0.17	0.04
z	3.08	0.67	1.06	0.49	-0.39	1.58	2.94	1.99	0.20	0.06
IIMAL										
z^*	-1.67	0.07	-2.17	-0.62	-1.02	-1.08	-0.23	-1.35	0.83	0.15
z	-2.28	0.08	-2.18	-0.65	-1.26	-1.30	-0.27	-1.74	1.00	0.20
GAZA										
z^*	-2.45	-0.72	-0.54	0.18	-2.16	-1.64	-1.65	-0.50	1.05	0.14
z	-3.26	-0.89	-0.51	0.19	-2.62	-1.96	-1.98	0.63	1.25	0.21
LKOH										
z^*	4.46	4.07	1.12	1.82	1.15	2.55	2.43	0.75	1.51	0.64
z	6.03	5.03	1.20	1.92	1.38	2.93	2.97	0.91	1.82	0.95
IRGZ										
z^*	1.67	-0.21	-0.99	-0.33	-1.09	2.32	2.29	-0.25	1.49	-0.24
z	2.24	-0.27	-1.00	-0.35	-1.33	2.61	2.74	-0.27	1.79	-0.38
MSNG										
z^*	3.97	1.80	-0.12	1.80	4.06	1.84	0.61	2.04	1.72	0.91
z	5.31	2.28	-0.12	1.90	5.04	1.99	0.76	2.42	2.07	1.46
FESH										
z^*	-6.37	0.70	-0.97	-1.67	-0.53	-1.53	-0.87	-2.95	-2.73	0.19
z	-8.70	0.89	-1.02	-1.76	-0.65	-1.87	-1.04	-3.87	-3.30	0.28
EESR										
z^*	2.87	1.63	0.80	-0.21	-0.21	0.59	1.46	2.03	2.12	1.32
z	3.85	1.96	0.82	-0.22	-0.25	0.66	1.77	2.26	2.50	2.05
LENE										
z^*	4.21	-0.07	-0.54	-2.22	-2.07	6.30	-0.05	3.07	2.93	1.20
z	5.63	-0.08	-0.56	-2.35	-2.57	6.43	-0.06	3.83	3.48	1.92
Index										
z^*	6.21	4.20	2.83	1.91	1.47	2.26	1.77	1.49	3.26	0.21
z	8.40	5.22	2.95	2.01	1.92	2.66	2.13	1.82	3.90	0.32

z indicates the homoscedasticity-consistent z-test, z^* indicates the heteroscedasticity-consistent z^*-test, at the 5% significance level scores exceeding +/-1.96 are significantly different from 1, and thus indicate the rejection of the random walk. All tests are based on first-order differences.

VII.B.   Evolving relative market efficiency over time

Besides analyzing the relationship between relative market efficiency and the transparency of securities, it is useful to look at how relative market efficiency behaves over time in a frontier equity market such as Russia. As indicated in chapter 5, price predictability is often a sign of an uneven playing field, where informed local investors profit at the expense of uninformed foreign investors. Eventually those uninformed foreign investors may decide to abstain from such a market and thus reduce liquidity and depth.[11] In this section, an assessment will be made of whether Russia has been moving in such a direction during the initial years of the Russian Trading System (RTS), or whether relative market efficiency was actually improving.

VII.B.1.   Results confirming improving relative market efficiency over time

Chart 7.0., which depicts both the homoscedasticity- and the heteroscedasticity consistent z-test statistics (z^*-test statistics) of the Rinaco Plus USD Russian equity index measured in equally-spaced time periods of 73 trading days resulting in nine periods, indicates a growing acceptance of the random walk over time. This trend, however, is sharply interrupted during the two major rallies (election rally and January 1997 rally in the Russian equity market).[12]

---

[11] Foreign investors are likely to shun investment opportunities in markets which display strong insider trading behavior (see Czech Republic between 1997 and early 1999). In the event of severe macroeconomic instability and currency risk, observed relative market efficiency or inefficiency becomes secondary in the decision-making process of foreign investors. The case of Russia in autumn 1998, presents the best example of how severe forms of currency risk can eliminate a frontier equity market entirely from the map of investment opportunities for foreign investors. Accordingly, the analyses presented here are applicable during periods of macro-economic stability or improvement. In other cases, the risk of currency devaluation or hyperinflation and prohibitively high interest rates are far more relevant in determining the investment opportunities.

[12] Please refer to chart 3.0. in chapter 3, which depicts the Russian equity index.

Chart 7.0. Variance ratio test statistics of USD Russian Equity Index (Rinaco Plus) measured over nine equally-spaced time periods from January 1995 to September 1997

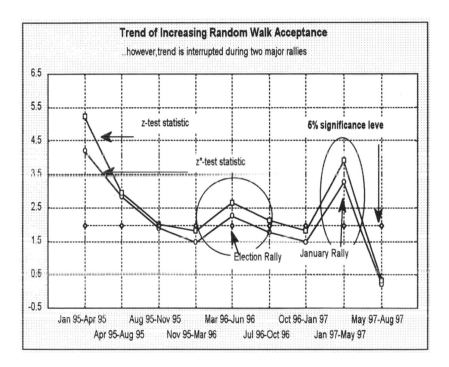

During the weeks of the two rallies, the Russian equity market was overwhelmingly driven by foreign investors. This fact, in itself, can lead to a similar argumentation as in part VII.A., and thus would serve as an explanation of why the random walk is assaulted. There is however, a second argument which was expressed by New York-based brokerages dealing in Russian equities. During the post-rally phases, or alternatively expressed, during market corrections (which have succeeded both the election- and the January-rally), many Moscow-based brokers and virtually all smaller brokerages are avoided in transactions, as their counterparty risk is deemed too high when the market retreats excessively, and the option of pre-payment is generally not available or not practiced. As long as there is no central clearing mechanism in place, this situation is not expected to change.[13] This situation hinders the quick and accurate price creation

---

[13] Harvey Sawikin, "The Russian Stock Market: First-Rank or Second-Rate?" *The Russian* (December/January 1998): 24.

process. Transactions that would or should take place, and for which there are bid and ask quotes, are not conducted for counterparty risk-based reasons. Consequently, prices remain sticky at an artificial level for some time.

A last, and a somewhat weaker argument could be made on the basis of so-called stealth trading. Stealth trading implies that large funds need several days when liquidating positions in thin markets (hence autocorrelated moments would be introduced), without risking to drive down the price. This situation normally does not arise during the purchasing process, as pre-emerging market purchases are often done after brokers suggest they have a substantial block of shares available. Moreover, equity entry points in frontier markets are more widely spread in time than exit points, which often are a result of major news flow items which unfavorably affect the market.[14]

In conclusion of the results presented in VII.A. and VII.B., it can be said that (a) less dedicated investors currently face a market which is characterized by a lower degree of relative market efficiency in those securities in which they participate, and (b) the overall Russian equity market displays a degree of improving relative market efficiency between early 1995 and late 1997. The risk of foreign mainstream investors retreating from Russia because of relative market efficiency-based reasons, therefore does not seem excessive. Mainstream investors are still trading the Russian market and will eventually broaden their exposure as liquidity and transparency will rise, and will promote more securities into the universe of investable equities for a larger segment of the market – this is if macro-economic stability resurfaces. This development will dilute the market segmentation which still prevails and overall gradually shift the Russian market bit by bit to the level where it becomes economical to specialize in this market and hire dedicated Russia analysts - even for non-dedicated international equity funds. Finally, Russia should rival such large, deep, resilient, liquid and mature emerging markets such as Mexico. The macroeconomic shock caused by the Ruble devaluation of 1998 put this process on hold for some time.

[14] Richard W. Sias and Laura T. Strarks, " Return autocorrelation and institutional investors," *Journal of Financial Economics* 46 (1997): 103-131.

Chapter 8

ADRs and GDRs - International Depository Receipts in Frontier Markets
King-makers in frontier markets

The rise of depository receipt programs has affected both local emerging markets and international investors. Local emerging market issuers have found a quick and painless entry into the investable universe of global equities, and therewith absorbed many of the benefits, such as higher liquidity and thinner bid-ask spreads, which are characteristic of widely traded instruments. For the investor, depository receipt program-sponsors have rolled out the red carpet to less dedicated international fund managers, who in pre-depository receipt times, would not have ventured into many countries' markets of which their portfolios now contain depository receipts backed by local shares (see chart 8.0.).[1]

In the context of this book, depository receipts form a well-suited transition from the questions related to evolving relative market efficiency of the preceding chapters to the topic of the next chapter which will address methods of valuing frontier market equities. The relevance of depository receipts can be fittingly categorized in this dual context: Do depository receipts affect the relative efficiency of the local equity market, and to what extent do depository receipt programs display a new dimension of informational inefficiency which could be profitably exploited by the investor who precisely times purchases of underlying shares according to the schedule of depository receipts?

The first question of whether increased relative market efficiency can be attributed to the rise of depository receipt programs cannot be

[1] In 1996, 38% of all new forms of ADRs came from emerging markets.

unambiguously answered in the affirmative.   As we have seen in the previous chapter, the top-transparency portfolio, which largely consists of

Chart 8.0.   Holdings of ADRs vs local shares 1996

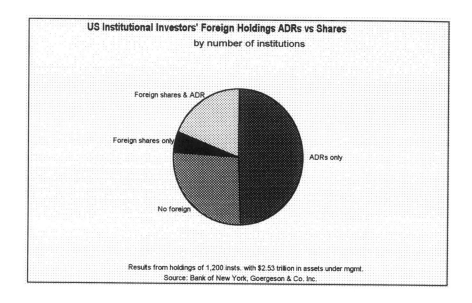

shares with depository receipt programs in place, does not fare well on the score of relative market efficiency.   On the other hand, shares with global depository receipts in place clearly have shown the thinnest bid/ask spreads (see table 8.8).

The second question relating to the investor and unexploited profit-making opportunities, as well opens a more complex view than often assumed by foreign investors who claim to profitably 'ride the ADR wave', or 'play the ADR game'.[2]   Although the tests conducted in this chapter reveal that investors can benefit from buying local shares on first rumors of an ADR listing, a closer examination on the other hand suggests that there are sizable differences among underlying shares and their reaction to impending depository receipt facilities.   Thus a more inquisitive approach

---

[2] The term 'riding the ADR wave' represents an investment strategy in frontier emerging markets which bases the stock selection on the likelihood of companies' plans to sponsor depository receipt facilities and thus enhance the liquidity and transparency of the underlying securities. This, in turn, often implies a higher level of investment inflows into the securities and hence price appreciation following the initial depository receipt trading date.

questioning the factors motivating the issuance of depository receipt programs is always adequate and prudent.

VIII.A.   Definition and benefits of ADRs and GDRs

American Depository Receipts (ADRs) are US dollar-denominated negotiable instruments issued in the US by a depository bank.[3] The holder of an ADR enjoys ownership of non-US securities. Those securities are normally referred to as the local or underlying shares. ADRs and Global Depository Receipts (GDRs) are identical from a legal, technical and administrative point of view. The word "Global" is occasionally preferred for marketing reasons. Non-US listed depository receipts are usually referred to as GDRs.

In mid-1997, approximately 1,600 depository receipt programs for companies from over 60 countries existed.[4] While many depository receipts are listed in the US, UK or Germany, the cross-listing of shares is practiced virtually across the globe. The non-native market often takes on the primary role in trading specific securities if the company's home market does not fashion a liquid or well-organized exchange. In this context, many Chinese (mainland) companies were traded in Hong Kong (when it was still under British auspices), some Estonian shares trade in Finland, some Russian shares trade in Latvia, and many African shares trade at regionally 'pooled' exchanges that are more active than their national exchanges. Of the emerging markets, no other region has taken ADR issuance to the same extreme as Latin America. In March 1995, 87%, 54%, 62%, and 71% of the domestic indices in Mexico, Argentina, Chile, and Brazil, respectively, could be traded as ADRs in the US.[5]

Depository receipts programs offer several attractive characteristics for the issuing company and the investor.

The main benefits to the company are:

1. Creation of a larger market for its shares and a more diversified shareholder base, which should both stabilize the share price and provide

---

[3] For Russian depository receipts, The Bank of New York has the clear monopoly as it has structured virtually every Russian depository receipts program.
[4] Source: The Bank of New York
[5] Kent Hargis, "The Globalization of Trading and Issuance of Equities from Emerging Markets," *The Journal of Emerging Markets,* vol 2, no 1 (Spring 1997): 5-21.

additional liquidity, which in turn decreases the illiquidity discount for many companies.

2. Enhancement of the company's image in the international market place-a process which feeds back into marketing of its products and its attractiveness as a workplace.   More importantly, depending on the specific type of depository receipt program (unsponsored, Level 1, 2, or 3), the company is obliged to disclose a degree of financial information that it would not have to disclose in its local market. This benefits the company as it often requires professional audits, professional corporate finance intermediaries (such as a Western investment bank), and generally a higher degree of reporting and shareholder information transparency, which raises the profile and the attractiveness of the company from the investor's perspective.

3. A mechanism for raising additional capital if the local market cannot absorb a new, or a secondary equity issue. This is often the case in emerging markets, where equity distribution infrastructure is in an infant stage on the institutional, as well as on the retail side, or where fixed income markets exhibit a relatively more attractive investment profile than the local equity market.

The main benefits to the investor are equally important. Obstacles such as unreliable custody and settlement in a foreign country (particularly frontier emerging markets), costly currency conversions, and opaque tax conventions may all impose barriers to investing in international securities.

Specifically the main benefits of depository receipts to investors are:

1. Depository receipts are usually quoted in dollars (or in DM and sterling if issued as GDRs in Europe). Dividends (or interest in the case of bonds) are paid in dollars.

2. Depository receipts serve as the best way to overcome burdens imposed by compliance departments in investment management institutions which may have restrictions on the purchase of securities outside their domestic market.

3. Global custody safekeeping charges are eliminated, thus allowing depository receipts holders to save between 10 to 40 basis points annually.

4. Depository receipts are as liquid as the underlying shares since the two
    are interchangeable (two-way fungibility), but trading may be
    asymmetrically concentrated in local or ADR shares.

VIII.A.1. Four types of depository receipt programs

A company can choose among four types of depository receipt programs: an
unsponsored depository receipt program, and three types of sponsored
depository receipt programs. Unsponsored programs have become less
popular as the company lacks control over the facility and there are
numerous hidden costs associated with such programs. Unsponsored
facilities are created as a reaction to market demand. In those cases one or
several depository banks decide to purchase securities and issue depository
receipts against them. Unsponsored receipts are not accompanied by a
formal agreement with the company. As an increasing number of
companies, for which there is demand for depository receipts, issues
sponsored receipt facilities in pursuance of some of the above mentioned
goals (raise new capital, transparency, liquidity), the potential number of
companies qualifying for unsponsored receipt facilities is dwindling rapidly.

VIII.A.2. Sponsored Level-I depository receipts

A sponsored Level-I depository receipt facility is usually the first and easiest
way for any company to access the international capital markets. In the US,
Level-I depository receipts are traded over-the-counter (OTC) and cannot be
listed on a national exchange such as AMEX, NYSE, or NASDAQ. Outside
the US they are occasionally traded OTC and on some exchanges (e.g.
Berlin, LSE, OTC bulletin board).

What makes Level-I depository receipt programs attractive entry vehicles
are the lax disclosure requirements. The company does not need to comply
with US Generally Accepted Accounting Principles (US GAAP) or full
Securities and Exchange Commission (SEC) disclosure. Hence, the company
benefits from access to international capital markets without having to
change its reporting standards.

When entering into a depository agreement with a depository bank in the
US, the responsibilities of the depository bank include mailing annual

reports, maintaining shareholder records, and responding to investor inquiries.[6]

Table 8.0. Sponsored Level-I Depository Receipts

SEC Registration	Form F-6 (1933 Securities Act) 12g3-(b) exemption (1934 Exchange Act)
Advantages	Build core group of investors/no SEC disclosure/easy/low cost/ control
Disadvantages	Limited visibility/cannot raise capital or list on a national exchange
Investors	All US investors and non-US investors
Listing	OTC 'pink sheet' and electronic bulletin board
Settlement	T+3, DTC, Euroclear, CEDEL
Cost	$25,000 or less
Application	Non-US companies wishing to develop foreign shareholder base without significant cost or SEC involvement

Source: The Bank of New York and Brunswick Brokerage

VIII.A.3. Sponsored Level-II depository receipts

The sponsored Level-II depository receipt program differs from sponsored Level-I programs as it allows the company to list its depository receipts on an exchange in the U.S. and on some exchanges outside the U.S. A public offering is not permitted under the Level-II program. The company must comply with all the SEC registration and reporting requirements, including the submission of annual reports in accordance with US GAAP.

---

[6] Kent Hargis, "The Globalization of Trading and Issuance of Equities from Emerging Markets," *The Journal of Emerging Markets,* vol 2, no 1 (Spring 1997): 5-21.
Further information on depository receipt programs can be obtained from:
The Bank of New York, *Global Offering of Depository Receipts-A Transaction Guide*
Corporate Trust & Agency Group-Bankers Trust Company – *Depository Receipts*

Table 8.1. Sponsored Level-II Depository Receipts

SEC Registration	Form F-6 (1933 Securities Act) Forms 20-F and 6K (1934 Exchange Act)
Advantages	Listing/High visibility/Liquidity
Disadvantages	Full SEC disclosure/Continuous reporting cost
Investors	All US investors and non-US investors
Listing	NASDAQ, AMEX, NYSE, Non-US exchanges
Settlement	T+3, DTC, Euroclear, CEDEL
Cost	$200,000-$700,000
Application	Non US companies wishing to raise the visibility and enhance the liquidity of their shares without public offering

Source: The Bank of New York and Brunswick Brokerage

VIII.A.4. Sponsored Level-III depository receipts

While Level-I and Level-II depository receipts use existing shares to enhance the shareholder base, Level-III depository receipts issuers can raise capital through public placement. As with Level-II and Level-III facilities, institutional and retail investors can participate in these programs. Moreover, a three-year history of US GAAP compliant accounts is required in order to file Form 20-F. In young emerging markets, Level-III depository facilities have been less numerous as the three-year US GAAP accounts requirement remains the main obstacle. However, Level-I and II issuers are frequently inclined to upgrade to a Level-III facility.

Table 8.2. Sponsored Level-III Depository Receipts

SEC Registration	Form F-1 and F-6 (1933 Securities Act) Forms 20-F and 6 K (1934 Exchange Act)
Advantages	Raise capital/Listing/Maximum visibility and liquidity
Disadvantages	Full SEC disclosure/Continuous reporting cost
Investors	All US investors and non-US investors
Listing	NASDAQ, AMEX, NYSE, Non-US exchanges
Settlement	T+3, DTC, Euroclear, CEDEL
Cost	$500,000-$2,000,000, plus underwriter's margin
Application	Non-US companies wishing to raise capital (from $40,000,000 for countries with few or no regulations preventing foreign investment)

Source: The Bank of New York and Brunswick Brokerage

VIII.A.5. Private placements – 144A and Reg S

Rule 144A depository receipts are privately placed receipts which are issued and traded in accordance with Rule 144A. Reg S depository receipts can convert to Level-I facilities after 40 days. The major advantages are:[7]

1. More cost effective than an exchange listing when raising capital.

2. Minimized SEC reporting (utilizing the reporting exemption under 12g3-2(b) and 144(d).

3. Over 4,000 qualified institutional buyers (QIBs) and other institutional buyers permitted to trade these securities.

4. US GAAP reconciliation of financial statements not required.

---

[7] Source: Bankers Trust Company – Corporate Trust & Agency Group marketing presentation

The main disadvantages are:

1. Rule 144A depository receipts cannot be created for classes of shares already listed on a US exchange.

2. Rule 144A depository receipts can only be sold in the US to other QIBs.

3. The QIB market is not as liquid as the public US equity market.

Table 8.3.   Private Placements 144A and Regulation "S"

Description	Private placement in the US to QIBs[8]
Purpose	Sell shares to raise capital through private placement; Reg S can convert to Level-I after 40 days
Customers	144A: Institutional only (QIB) Reg S: Institutional and retail
Trading	OTC
SEC Registration	None
US Reporting	Need comprehensive offering memorandum
Other Requirements	Exemption under Rule 12g3-2(b), or Rule 144A (d4)

Source: The Bank of New York and Brunswick Brokerage

---

[8] A QIB is currently defined as an institution which owns and invests on a discretionary basis at least US$ 100 million (or, in the case of registered broker-dealers, US$ 10 million) in securities of an unaffiliated entity. At present there are in excess of 4000 QIBs but the SEC may decide to broaden the definition of a QIB to allow a larger number to participate in the Rule 144A market. Non-US companies now have easy access to the US equity private placement market and may thus raise capital through the issue of restricted ADRs without conforming to the full SEC registration and reporting requirements. Additionally, the cost of issuing 144As is considerably less than the cost of initiating a Sponsored Level III ADR program. (source: Deutsche Bank).

VIII.B. The Russian case of depository receipt facilities

VIII.B.1.   Description of Russian depository receipt facilities

Table 8.4. depicts the Russian depository receipts analyzed for the frontier market case study of Russia. While a small number of banks exist which have sponsored depository programs, those are not considered for this case study as insufficient data are publicly available for the relevant time periods, and foreign investors faced investment barriers, which did not allow them to invest in Russian financial institutions until recently. The commonly accepted explanation of why Russian financial institution sponsored depository programs revolves primarily around marketing-related reasons.[9]

Table 8.4. Russian depository receipt programs[10]

Company	Sector	Type of ADR	Issue date	Exchange/listing
Chernogorneft	Oil/gas	Level 1	3/22/96	Berlin/OTC
Gazprom	Oil/gas	144A/Reg S	10/24/96	Berlin/LSE
GUM	Retail	Level 1	6/7/96	Berlin/OTC
Irkutskenergo	Utility	Level 1	1/23/97	Berlin/OTC
LUKoil (common)	Oil/gas	Level 1	12/31/95	Berlin/OTC
Mosenergo	Utility	144A/Reg S	10/13/95	Berlin/Portal
Surgutneftegas	Oil/gas	Level 1	12/30/96	Berlin/OTC
Tatneft	Oil/gas	144A/Reg S	11/29/96	Berlin/LSEP

Source: Salomon Brothers

In May 1997, three companies - LUKoil, Mosenergo, and Gazprom - represented almost 84% of the total market capitalization of all Russian ADRs. At the same time, total Russian ADR market capitalization represented 7% of the Russian market's total capitalization.[11] As a comparison, in Mexico, one of the leading ADR issuers in emerging

---

[9] Inkombank, Bank Menatep, and Bank Vozrozhdeniye had sponsored Level-I ADRs in 1996. The issue of Seversky Tube Works and Vimpelcom are not considered for data insufficiency reasons and because of the nature of the firms (Vimpelcom had an initial public offering at the NYSE and was not considered a genuine Russian company by many -due to valuation and management, and its non-listed status in Russia), respectively.

[10] Data as of early 1997. The total number of Russian depository receipts more than doubled during 1997.

[11] Salomon Brothers

markets, ADRs accounted for 14.1% of total market capitalization in 1996. This demonstrated a rapid increase from only 1.8% in 1989.[12] In 1996, Russia (5.23%) followed Brazil (7.3%), Hong Kong (11.64%) and the UK (16.75%) in the top list of new sponsored depository receipts issued by country.[13]

Except for Gazprom depository receipts, there are no restrictions imposed on converting local shares into ADRs.[14] In the case of Gazprom, the company's charter limits the amount of shares to be held by foreigners in ADR form to 9%. After the first international depository receipt issue, about 2% of the shares were held by foreigners.

Frontier market case study

Gazprom – attempted ringfence assault

The case of Gazprom has come under close international scrutiny when foreign arbitrageurs in February 1997 intended to assault the ringfence by accumulating local stock which then was to be synthetically transformed into ADR equivalents. Due to the company's charters which prohibited foreigners from buying local Gazprom shares, the ADRs traded at up to a 75% premium to the local shares. The synthetic ADR creation by the arbitrageurs, especially by the Hong Kong-based Regent Pacific, which intended to use $200 million worth of local Gazprom stock as collateral for shares in the specially created Russian legal entity "Regent Gaz Fund", would have been a source of fabulous profits. However, Gazprom management, with full backing of the Russian government, deterred via some opaque measures, the arbitrage from continuing. In the meantime, the local share price appreciated rapidly, thus narrowing the ADR premium, and

---

[12] Bank of New York

[13] Bank of New York

[14] During 1996, arbitrage trading between Mexico's five largest ADRs and their underlying shares accounted for between 10%-15% of the total value traded in those firms' shares. Numbers for Russia are not available, but there is no reason to believe they should not be of a similar magnitude. This reflects the interdependence of underlying shares and ADR shares.

indicating that at least in the minds of market participants, the arbitrage was on.

Analysts are still speculating why foreign arbitrageurs were tacitly allowed to pursue their agenda to a degree that helped the local share price appreciate, and thus enrich holders of the local shares, which among others were managers of Gazprom itself. The other lesson that somewhat defeats traditional finance theory is that Gazprom actually managed to charge foreign shareholder three times as much for its shares as the local price dictated at the time, and still achieved a massive oversubscription of the ADR offering.

This is a classic case of market segmentation in frontier markets. The initial market segmentation mechanism finally was assaulted, and the costs were incurred by foreign investors who participated in the international depository receipt offering. At the same time, the regulatory authorities were undermined along with Russian corporate governance and the regulatory basis of the Russian securities market in general. The frustration of foreign investors finally translated into a deeper valuation discount for Russian equities versus their peers from other frontier emerging markets.

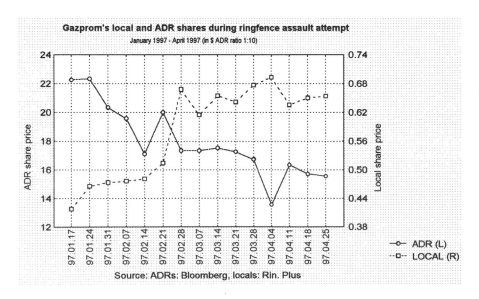

For further information refer to Financial Times and Wall Street Journal during February 1997, both fashioned explicit and frequent coverage of the case.

In order to understand the relationship between ADRs and underlying shares, it helps to demonstrate in simplified terms how ADR arbitrage is

executed.   Box 8.0. describes a plain-vanilla ADR arbitrage with the
example of LUKoil shares.   The ratio of underlying shares to ADRs is 4:1
(referred to as ADR ratio).   It must be noted that the cost items in Russian
ADR arbitrage are (1) a conversion charge of 5 cents per ADR, that is
charged by the Bank of New York, which has a monopoly on Russian
ADRs, and (2) a re-registration fee of 3 cents per share, that has to be paid if
the arbitrage executing institution does not source from, and does not feed
back the shares into its own books.

To initiate a plain-vanilla arbitrage, a trader could purchase 4 underlying
shares of LUKoil common stock.   For purposes of illustration, the price the
trader pays per share would be $18.   At this point the trader owns 4 shares of
LUKoil common stock.   The next step would be to convert the 4 shares into
1 ADR (remember, the ADR ratio was 4:1).   The depository bank would
charge a fee of $0.05 per conversion.   Following the conversion, a re-
registration has to take place if the shares are not coming and going back to
the institution's own books, in other words, if a client is involved in the
arbitrage. After this transaction, the trader owns one share of LUKoil ADRs
which has an implicit cost attached to it of $72.17.

In order to make a profit, the trader now has to find a counterparty who
would quote a bid of more than $72.17 per LUKoil ADR.   If an arbitrage
was at place, this bid had been quoted prior to commencing the arbitrage
(this is why *arbitrage* ≈ riskless profit).

The arbitrage between depository receipts and underlying shares
ascertains that despite different demand and supply schedules locally and
internationally, the price difference between the depository receipt and the
underlying shares remains too small to make a consistent profit after
transaction costs.   There are cases when the depository receipts trade at a
consistent premium or discount to the local shares (Korean ADRs).   In such
cases, other risk factors such as tax laws, foreign ownership limits on local
shares, or liquidity constraints are the reason for the deviation from parity-
pricing.

Another case, which exemplifies the virtues of depository receipts are
special basket structures which are created by the derivatives departments of
emerging market brokers.   Such structures are traded in the US and often
derive their value from a number of securities which would be too illiquid if
bought individually, and too costly to trade if bought locally.   One prominent
example has been the Russian regional telecommunication basket which was

designed during 1996 by a major US investment bank. This structure
provided a participation conduit into regional Russian telecommunications
for international investors, who otherwise would have been limited to
relatively liquid Russian telecommunications shares such as Rostelekom,
Vimpelcom, etc.

Box 8.0. Simplified mechanism of ADR/underlying share arbitrage

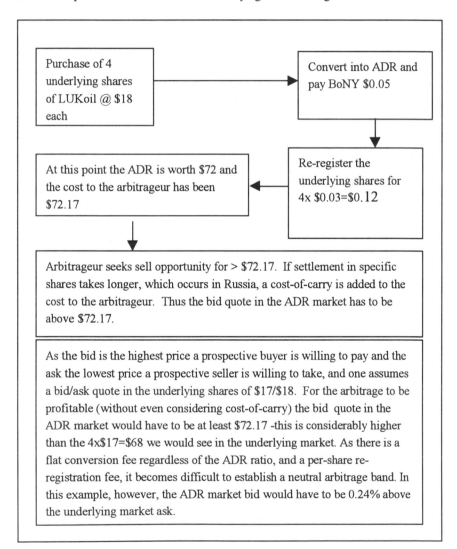

VIII.B.2. Trading trends in Russian ADRs

Table 8.5. shows the process of transformation of local shares into ADR form subsequent to the issuance of ADRs. The longer the ADR has been in place, the higher the share of free float in ADR form.[15] For issues with a 12 month history of ADRs, the amount of free floating stock in ADR form is between 20% and 58%. For more recent ADRs such as Surgutneftegas and Irkutskenergo, which issued ADRs in December 1996 and January 1997, respectively, the ADRs comprise between 10% and 16% of total free float. This trend clearly indicates the strong foreign influence on shares with depository receipt facilities in place.

Table 8.5.   Percentage of shares outstanding in ADRs and free float

Percentage of shares in ADRs and free float (Dec 95- March 97) in %							
	Dec 95	March 96	June 96	Sep 96	Dec 96	Mar 97	Free float
Mosenergo	4.0	23.1	25.0	28.0	28.0	28.6	49.0
LUKoil		20.6	21.0	22.7	22.7	22.7	77.5
Chernogorneft		14.7	17.2	10.9	10.9	12.8	62.3
GUM		3.1	15.3	20.9	20.9	27.4	100.0
Tatneft			0.8	13.9	13.9	17.8	36.4
Gazprom				2.0	2.0	2.0	51.9
Surgutneftegas						7.49	49.0
Irkutskenergo						5.92	60.0

Source: Salomon Brothers

As foreign participation increases when ADRs are issued, trading volume rises and liquidity is equally enhanced (see table 8.6.) This in turn translates into tighter bid/ask spreads for the local (or underlying) shares which make profit-generating arbitrage between differing quotes by different brokers increasingly difficult (see table 8.7.).

---

[15] Free float counts the number of shares of a corporation that are outstanding and available for trading by the public. A small free float number usually implies more volatility in the share price since a large buy/sell order can have a more dramatic impact on the share price.

Table 8.6.   Trading volumes for Russian ADRs and local shares in 1996

Company	ADR market (USD)	Local market (USD)	ADR % of local market
Mosenergo	235,947,517	545,471,865	43
LUKoil	897,998,092	347,671,311	258
Chernogorneft	82,792,755	34,270,652	242
GUM	17,391,315	48,872,230	36
Gazprom	446,891,580	110,123,900	406
Seversky Tube Works	19,524,361	13,731,395	142
Tatneft	35,586,523	20,871,332	171
TOTAL	1,736,132,143	1,121,012,684	155

Table 8.7.   Average bid/ask spread of local Russian shares with ADRs in 1996

ADR issuer	1 Qtr	2 Qtr	3 Qtr	4 Qtr
Chernogorneft	15.2%	10.6%	26.1%	9.7%
Gazprom	126.2%	327.5%	36.2%	6.1%
GUM	29.6%	10.6%	9.9%	10.2%
Irkutskenergo	9.6%	5.3%	5.8%	4.1%
LUKoil	3.0%	2.4%	1.9%	1.0%
Mosenergo	1.3%	1.7%	1.1%	0.6%
Seversky Tube	64.1%	54.2%	36.1%	17.4%
Surgutneftegas	15.8%	10.8%	3.4%	1.5%
Tatneft	126.8%	82.0%	72.3%	7.6%

Source: Salomon Brothers and RTS, NASD, NYSE, LSE, and BSE. The reported ADR volumes may only represent a small share of total ADR trading, nevertheless, they still outweigh trading volume in local shares. Spreads are calculated by taking the difference between the bid and offer price and dividing it by the mean of the bid and offer price.

While table 8.7. demonstrates the dynamic aspect of spread tightening of local shares with ADRs, table 8.8. clearly shows that ADRs' bid-ask spreads are considerably tighter than those of shares without depository receipts facilities in place. The exceptions are UES and Rostelekom, which, as Russia's 'blue chips', trade at comparable spreads to the shares with depository receipts.

Table 8.8.   Average bid/ask spread November 1997

Company (ADRs bold)	November 1997 average bid/ask spread in %	Company (ADRs bold)	November 1997 average bid/ask spread in %
Aeroflot	13.1	Norilsk Nickel	7.2
Bashkirenergo	12.1	Novolipetsk Fer.Metal	0.0
Chelyabenergo	29.2	Novorossiysk Sea Shipping	22.2
Chelyabinsksviazinform	10.5	Noyabrskneftegaz	7.8
Chernogorneft	**22.4**	Orenburgneft	18.2
Condpetroleum	82.1	Permenergo	34.0
Far Eastern Shipping	88.1	Primorsk Sea Shipping	63.3
GAZ Auto Plant	5.7	Purneftegaz	7.3
Inkombank	15.9	Rostelecom	1.1
Irkutskenergo	**3.6**	Sakhalinmorneftegas	17.7
KamAZ	18.5	Samaraenergo	26.1
Komineft	45.5	Samaraneftegas	93.0
Krasnoyarskenergo	21.3	Samarasvyasinform	34.3
Krasny Octyabr	35.6	Sberbank of Russia	2.1
Kubanelektrosvyaz	16.9	Severstal	51.8
Kuzbasenergo	8.9	St.Pb. Telephone	23.6
Lenenergo	17.0	**Surgutneftegaz**	**2.5**
LUKoil	**0.4**	Sverdlovskenergo	19.3
Megionneftegaz	8.8	**Tatneft**	**2.0**
Moscow Telephone	10.3	Tomskneft	14.8

Source: Skatepress, Russia

Table 8.8. Average bid/ask spread November 1997 (continued)

Company (ADRs bold)	November 1997 average bid/ask spread in %	Company (ADRs bold)	November 1997 average bid/ask spread in %
Moscow Telephone	10.3	Tomskneft	14.8
Mosenergo	**0.5**	Trade House GUM	11.3
Nizhnevartovskneftegaz	62.0	Unified Energy System (UES)	0.3
Nizhniy Tagil Fer.Metal	26.5	Uralsviazinform	27.8
Nizhnovsvyazinform	24.9	Varegannefttegaz	123.1
YUKOS	10.0	Yuganskneftegaz	10.9

Source: Skatepress, Russia

VIII.B.3. Post-ADR issuance performance of underlying shares

A notorious trick, if one believes most brokers of Russian equities, has been to buy the underlying, or local, shares just before the ADRs are issued, or officially announced. This would enable the investor to benefit from the liquidity enhancement that is attributed to the issuance of international depository receipts, which in turn would narrow the illiquidity discount and thus increase the price of underlying shares.

This mechanism is logical as it relates to fundamental issues of share price formation. The decrease of the illiquidity discount, the diversification of the shareholder base, and the increased transparency which accompanies the regulatory requirements of international depository receipt programs, are all factors which in theory should help to enhance the intrinsic value of the underlying shares.

Finally, the issuance of depository receipts opens the market to a wider universe of investors and hence a deeper pool of capital. This translates directly into a flow-of-funds argument, which also should raise the underlying shares' price (see diagram 8.0.).

Diagram 8.0.   Effect of international depository receipt on local share price

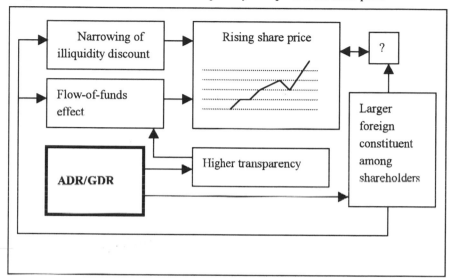

The discussion is still open on whether a larger international investor base, which supposedly purchases the international depository receipts, necessarily implies a rise in the share price. An argument, which is based on the belief that increased foreign ownership may expose the share price to sudden fluctuations as the top-down perception of a country demands rapid asset withdrawals or allocations, may be a valid one. Following such an argumentation, the above mentioned trading strategy may not necessarily be as plausibly explained as previously indicated.

There arguably have been cases when foreign investors over time have become the dominant force in trading the shares of a company that has issued ADRs, and where foreign investors have applied different - often less optimistic - valuation criteria to companies than the local shareholder base. In order to shed light upon what really happens in the pre-and post-depository receipt issuance phase, a simple analysis has been conducted.

VIII.B.4. Methodology for measuring share performance of pre-and post-ADR issuance in Russia

Ideally, the measurement of abnormal return is conducted with an event-study methodology. Such an approach could be described by the following methodology:[16] The event day zero is the ADR issue date and would be denoted as t=0. Common stock average abnormal returns are analyzed sixty days prior and sixty days post announcement date. The sixty day period is used as it reflects a fair forward-looking horizon for pre-emerging market investors. This means that even such ADR information which relates to ADR plans in the distant future, will in most cases not appear repeatedly in research reports as a buying flag until the more immediate time-horizon of approximately two months prior to the ADR issuance will have been reached.

The daily stock returns used in the formula would then be defined as:

(1)

$$R_{i,t} = \frac{P_{i,t} - P_{i,t-1}}{P_{i,t-1}}$$

where $P_{I,t}$ is the closing price on stock i at time t. In order to measure abnormal returns betas are computed. The beta reflects the covariance of the stock with an index. In this case it would be a Russian equity index. In addition to betas, alphas have to be computed. Alphas reflect the coefficient measuring the portion of a stock's return arising from specific, or non-market, risk. Betas of common stock are defined as:

(2)

$$\beta_t \equiv \frac{\sum_{i=1}^{n} (R_i - \overline{R_i})(R_M - \overline{R_M})}{\sum_{i=1}^{n} (R_M - \overline{R_M})^2}$$

[16] M. Ray, D. Thurston, and P. Dheeriya, "Effects of Seasoned Equity Issues in Emerging Markets: An Investigation in the Thai Stock Market," *The Journal of Emerging Markets*, vol. 1, no. 3 (Fall/Winter 1996): 22-34.

and alphas of common stocks are defined as:

(3)

$$\alpha_i \equiv \overline{R}_i - \beta_i \overline{R}_M$$

The alphas and betas are calculated from the stock and market index returns for the period 120 days to 60 days before the issuing date (i.e., from day − 120 to day −60), which is defined as the test period. The abnormal return for a depository receipt issuing firm is the deviation of its common stock's actual return from its predicted daily return. Abnormal returns are computed as follows:

(4)

$$A R_{i,t} \equiv R_{i,j} - (\alpha_i + \beta_{iR} R_{M,t})$$

The cumulative abnormal daily rate of return (CAR) from the beginning of the event period, day -60, to day 0 is defined as:

(5)

$$C A R^{0}_{-60} \equiv \sum_{t=-60}^{0} A R_t$$

This methodology, which has been successfully applied to other markets, fails in the context of a frontier equity market. The beta, which is required for the calculation of the abnormal rate of return is non-stationary.[17] This

---

[17] The problem of non-stationarity of betas has been known in emerging markets for many years. In one of his early articles, V.R. Errunza (V.R. Errunza, "Efficiency and the Brazilian Capital Market, " *Journal of Banking and Finance,* 3 (1979): 355-382.) points out the problem of non-stationary betas, and mitigates the effects by building portfolios of

means that the beta, which would be computed for the test period preceding the immediate pre-ADR issuance period, never remains close to the beta which can be calculated for the pre-ADR issuance, or post ADR issuance period. This raises the question of whether the beta itself becomes a function of the impending ADR issue. To answer this question, however, would be only of marginal interest to the practitioner of portfolio investment in frontier equity markets or the policy maker in Russian capital markets.

Alternative methods to adjust for the risk of the underlying assets when measuring its performance turn out to be equally futile.[18] Harvey (1995) and Bekaert (1995), in studies analyzing emerging market returns behavior, find that higher betas are often associated with lower returns. These findings reject traditional finance theory, but can be explained on the basis of market segmentation theory.[19] Furthermore, such results underline the futility of betas as risk-adjustment measures to compute abnormal return.

On a simpler note, the concept of the Capital-Asset-Pricing-Model (CAPM) and abnormal return is highly susceptible to criticism in frontier emerging markets. Methods intending to measure abnormal return, be it via a CAPM approach, or a regression against the index must at a minimum be based on the assumption that a *normal* return exists (we need a normal return in order to compute abnormal return). The fact is, that the Russian equity market, and for that matter, most frontier emerging markets, are characterized by only one constant and that would be 'change.' Whether it be in market segmentation dynamics, macro-economics, industry regulatory changes, fiscal policy, etc., the end result remains always that the outlook on equities and the universe of investors participating in the particular market or sector changes as well. This directly leads to the realization that a normal return, or alpha, cannot be reliably computed, because the assumption that equities display a stationary volatility versus their index cannot be upheld.

More importantly, however, an alternative methodology has to be found to assess the effect of issuing depository receipts on local share prices. While noting that a CAPM approach is not viable due to the previously

---

securities. Such an approach, which would increase the correlation over time for betas and thus establish quasi stationarity, is not applicable in this context as individual securities (ADRs) are the focus of interest.

[18] In chapter 3, the analysis of mean-variance frontiers gave inconclusive results as to whether securities with higher volatility generate higher returns. Therefore, adjusting for variance or standard deviation will not serve any purpose.

[19] Geert Bekaert and Campbell R. Harvey, "Time-varying world market integration," *Journal of Finance*, vol 50 (1995): 403-444.

mentioned reasons, the following methodology seems functional and robust
for assessing the above mentioned effect:
(6)

$$PIR = \frac{\displaystyle\sum_{i=1}^{60} P_i}{60} \Bigg/ \frac{\displaystyle\sum_{i=1}^{60} I_i}{60}$$

The price/index ratio is denoted by *PIR*, the absolute share price is denoted
by *P*, and the absolute value of the index is denoted by *I*. Therefore, the
average absolute price of the share is divided by the average absolute value
of the index over the same time period. The above defined formula
describes the computation of the ratio during the 60 day post-ADR issuance
period. The same ratio can be calculated according to the same method by
merely replacing the time period for the pre-ADR issuance period and the
period immediately preceding the pre-ADR issuance period. By comparing
the ratios of the individual time periods, an indication of relative
performance can be computed. The share prices and the index prices are
sourced from the Rinaco Plus brokerage in Moscow. [20]

---

[20] Composition and creation of Rinaco Plus Index:
The index is comprised of shares which are considered highly liquid on the Russian market.
The composition and calculation of the index rely heavily on expert estimations by the
RINACO Plus staff. Although it is not completely transparent, the RINACO Plus research
team exercises its best efforts to obtain timely, correct and consistent data. It is RINACO's
belief that the RES index, together with indices calculated by other parties, will provide an
accurate benchmark for the evaluation of market conditions. The exact and updated
composition of the index and the share prices can be downloaded on a daily basis from the
following web site:

http://www.fe.msk.ru/infomarket/rinacoplus/indicat/metod.html#3

VIII.B.5. Results of effects of depository receipts on share prices in Russia

Table 8.9. displays the absolute results obtained by applying the above mentioned methodology to the test time period (-120 to –60 days), the pre-ADR-period (-60 to 0 days), and the post-ADR period (0 to 60 days).

Table 8.9.   Relative performance of local shares before and after ADR issuance

	SNGS	CHGZ	GAZP	GUMM
pre-ADR -60 to –120 days	0.00297	0.074181	0.000988	0.096163
pre- ADR 60 days	0.00313	0.074717	0.003148	0.094151
post-ADR 60 days	0.00349	0.074377	0.002718	0.143245

	TATN	LKOH	IRGZ	Average
pre-ADR -60 to –120 days	0.165647	0.053832	1.000818	0.19923
pre- ADR 60 days	0.279394	0.047634	1.000986	0.21474
post-ADR 60 days	0.362437	0.058359	1.00124	0.23512

Table 8.10. shows the relative performance in percentage terms of the 60-day time periods immediately preceding and following the issuance date versus the 60-day "test" period. Here one can see that post-issuance periods show a stronger performance (average 18.02%) relative to the test period, than the time period immediately preceding the ADR issuance (average 7.78%). The fact that both periods, the pre-ADR and the post ADR period, outperform the test period in most cases, can be interpreted as the ADR having an economic effect on the security which is reflected in its price behavior during this time. Furthermore, the fact that the post-ADR period shows stronger performance than the pre-ADR period, suggests that the market prices the ADR characteristics into the local share price more aggressively after the announcement of the depository receipt program, than in the run-up phase leading to it. For investors this implies that although it generally pays off to keep the ADR watch bases on alert in order to be ready

to launch investments on the basis of ADR rumors, it is not too late to enter the market once the announcement has been made and the depository receipts have started trading.

Table 8.10. Relative performance of local shares before and after ADR issuance (in %) vs index

	SNGS	CHGZ	GAZP	GUMM
Pre-ADR 60 days	5.35%	0.72%	218.65%	-2.09%
Post- ADR 60 days	17.43%	0.26%	175.13%	48.96%

	TATN	LKOH	IRGZ	Average
Pre-ADR 60 days	68.67%	-11.51%	0.02%	7.78%
Post- ADR 60 days	118.80%	8.41%	0.04%	18.02%

When interpreting these results one must keep in mind that, although a degree of informational inefficiency can be attributed to these findings, the prudent investor should be careful in attributing these findings to economic inefficiency which could be profitably exploited. The sheer heterogeneity of companies issuing ADRs does not allow for a general framework of 'riding the ADR wave' in Russia. Some companies let it be known to investors 12-15 months prior to their actual issuing of depository receipts. Others move swiftly within one month or less of issuing the liquidity-enhancement instruments, and officially announce the ADR only days prior to their initial trading day. Some companies use the ADR primarily for marketing reasons and have little or no intention of upgrading a private placement or Level-I program to a Level-II or Level-III. Thus, the transparency benefits are capped and some of the virtues of ADR programs never come to work.

Therefore, ADR-based investments in local shares, despite their higher returns immediately before and after the issuance, must be analyzed one at a time and without relying to heavily on the mechanisms that are commonly called 'riding the ADR wave' in frontier markets.

The following guidelines may help to better understand the impact of ADRs on the local share price:

- What time line is the company envisioning for the issuance process?

- What is the purpose of the ADR (larger shareholder base, higher transparency, pure marketing, eventual upgrade to Level-III in order to raise capital abroad)?

- What type of investor relations program is in place?

VIII.B.6. Frontier market ADR fitness

As more ADRs will be launched in the Russian market and in other frontier emerging equity markets, the novelty will wear off and investors will increasingly assess ADRs according to the realization potential of the virtues that ADR programs possess. Thus, companies which seek transparency, liquidity and access to foreign capital raising venues (via the Level-III ADR), will most likely fare better than those that believe ADRs help to boost the share price in the short-term. In addition, the ADR factor will decreasingly take priority over the fundamentals of the company, as has happened in a number of cases in the past (see Gazprom example).

Moreover, ADR-sponsoring companies must increasingly be aware of the costs associated with ADRs. ADRs can become a painful burden if the pre-ADR shares were trading on the basis of benign local investor perceptions of the company. With a larger foreign constituent among shareholders, which in most cases has a substantially wider investment universe from which to select stocks, equity valuation will increasingly become a function of (a) their relative local market outlook versus other markets, and (b) their relative valuation versus their international industry sector peer groups.

Accordingly, depository receipt programs have to be critically assessed from the standpoint of the issuer and the standpoint of the investor. If the short-term goal of issuers is to boost the share price by adding ADRs to the stock's features, as it has been the case in Russia on not only one occasion, such an action would fall in the larger sphere of the 'greater fool' theory. There may be investors who are tantalized by the glossy announcements of ADRs (*those are the greater fools*). At the same time, however, there will now be more investors who will 'x-ray' the company behind it and possibly conclude that the upgrade to the international investment level requires operational efficiencies comparable to ADRs from other countries. Hence,

the issuer and the investor will have to decide on the company's ADR-
fitness before proceeding to this step.

Chapter 9

Valuation Approaches to Frontier Equity Markets
Search for the grail of frontier wisdom

Pre-emerging equity markets mostly do not enjoy the benefit of being thoroughly researched by a large number of sell-side security analysts. Moreover, security analysts covering pre-emerging markets may not be as experienced as their colleagues covering more mature emerging markets – particularly for those reasons spelled out in chapter 1. Their learning experience, in many cases, is a direct function of the age and maturing process of the frontier emerging market itself.[1] In addition to the lack or relative unreliability of equity coverage during the initial stages of the transformation from a pre-emerging market to a mature emerging market, accounting standards and audits can be characterized as having severe shortfalls in accuracy and standardization.

During the pre-emerging market stages, despite the partial presence of Western auditing firms, financial statements are still incompletely audited, and for the most part are neither historically restated to allow for meaningful comparisons, nor are they consolidated.[2] This situation raises the question: Does fundamental company data have any real value to the investor in the early stage of an equity market? The answer is a clear no. Any investment process which is based on fundamental data is doomed to fail if such data does not offer reliability and accuracy. Unless, however, the analytical investment process uses such data to draw flow of funds and market psychology-based conclusions about the frontier equity market. This requires laterally gauging the market by using all available information, by connecting the remaining dots, and by shrewdly drawing conclusions from

---

[1] This is particularly well demonstrated in chapter 1, chart 1.0.

[2] Please refer to the description of Russian accounting peculiarities in chapter 3.

behavioral finance patterns and from observing some fundamental rules of market segmentation theory.

IX.A.   Gauging the future performance of Russian equities during the early phase of the pre-emerging market life-cycle

IX.A.1. Description of the model

This chapter attempts to shed light upon the dynamic process of equity valuation in the Russian frontier equity market by testing a differentiated transparency-dynamic equity valuation approach over two time periods: the initial phase of the Russian equity market between mid-1995 to mid-1996, and the follow-up time period ranging from mid-1996 to mid-1997. The primary goal of the model is to test the viability of specific valuation measures, ranging from asset-based valuation ratios, such as market capitalization over reserves, market capitalization over production, market capitalization over capacity installed, or market capitalization over access lines, to financials-based measures, such as market capitalization over sales or earnings. Furthermore, a third measure is introduced: it will be called the technical parameter. This technical parameter - WAM- comprises less tangible but important characteristics of equities (see diagram 9.0.). WAM describes equity assessment in three categories: (1) degree of *W*estern audit, (2) degree of availability of *A*merican depository receipt program (ADR), and (3) size of *M*arket capitalization.

Fundamental measures and the technical indicator WAM are applied to both the early and the later periods. The later period (ranging from mid-1996 to mid-1997) differs from the earlier period in that the coverage and transparency has dramatically improved.[3] The time frame of the early Russian equity market lends itself uniquely to this analysis as the time period 1995-1996 represents the true genesis period of the market. Foreign investment was in its infant stage and research report coverage of the Russian equity market was extremely thin. The period 1996-1997, on the other hand, was the first period when Russian investments became mainstream and no single global fund could afford to ignore Russia's returns during 1996-97. Research coverage became abundant and investors around the globe learnt about individual Russian companies and their operations.

---

[3] See table 5.1. in chapter 5 for the cumulative broker report coverage of the most liquid companies. Table 5.1. shows the rapid rise in equity coverage during the period from mid-1996 to mid-1997.

This is also a stage that all large frontier emerging markets experience. During this post-genesis period many global investment banks offer research, set up local operations, and media and brokerage research coverage becomes intense. In addition, this is the period when most depository receipt programs are issued. As this is a stage that exists in most large frontier markets at one point, it is relevant to examine which valuation measures become most meaningful. For now let us call this stage the 'wake-up stage' of frontier equity markets. Matter-of-factly, this stage is also associated with high returns in frontier emerging equity markets, which in many cases are never matched in scale during subsequent stages of frontier and emerging market development.

Diagram 9.0.   Structure of transparency-dynamic valuation model

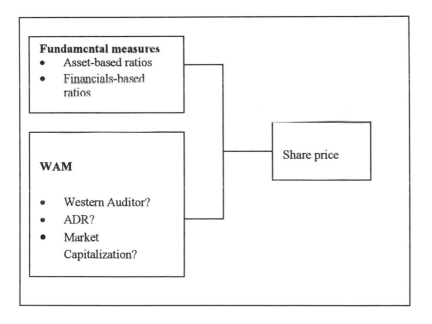

While this model will clarify aspects related to the choice of valuation measures as far as fundamental or technical parameters are concerned, it will not try to be conclusive about the valuation of equity securities in frontier emerging markets. The findings, thus will serve as a pre-screening tool which may help the investor to weed out the most unattractive securities, and select the group with the highest scores for further analysis. As timely decision-making in investment management is crucial, especially in markets where dramatic rallies sometimes last no longer than a few days, the pre-screening methodology can serve the investment professional well. The next step that must be taken is to analyze the securities, which have passed the screening test with the best results, according to the relevant measures and approaches for the specific industry.

IX.A.2. Data description

Table 9.0. below describes the ratios of fundamental criteria which were available to the investor during the period from mid-1995 to mid-1996. The accounting data is from the year 1994, which for many companies was the first year for which accounting data was available. While fragmented data was possibly available for individual companies for an earlier period, the small number of companies in the individual sectors would not have allowed for any meaningful statistical analysis. Furthermore, the analysis had to be limited to the three main sectors: oil/gas, electric utilities, and telecommunications. It was only in those sectors where a meaningful number of companies with accounting data for 1994 could be found. The sector limitation, however, does not pose a problem as those sectors attracted most investors' interest. Table 9.1. is composed according to the same methodology but uses 1995 accounting data. The universe of companies is somewhat larger as 1995 data was available for more companies than 1994 data.

IX.A.2.1. Agreeing on valuation parameters

The most notable observation from the fundamental valuation tables 9.0. and 9.1. are captured in chart 9.0. (found in appendix to chapter IX.). Chart 9.0. depicts the magnitude and the degree of dispersion of the individual valuation measures from the two time periods examined (mid-95 to mid-96 and mid-96 to mid-97). The degree of dispersion and the magnitude of asset-based measures (such as market capitalization/production, market capitalization/reserves, market capitalization/MW installed, or market capitalization/access lines) rises in the later time period. The larger values simply reflect higher valuations during the later period. This is to be expected. As companies grew and investors gained a higher degree of understanding of the market, more investors bought Russian equities in 1995 than in 1994. Accordingly, higher demand and limited supply drives up equity valuations.

The larger degree of dispersion of asset-based measures during the later testing period, however, suggests more a discriminating application of asset-based measures. This can be explained on the basis of investors learning about individual companies and investors' rising ability to rely to a larger degree on financial ratios during the later phase. This means that investors are increasingly applying financials-based measures, such as price/earnings, price/sales, and price/book value, which would render some of the more crude asset-based measures less relevant, and thus lead to a higher degree of dispersion of asset-based measures.

Table 9.0. Fundamental data 1994

Company	Mkt cap in $ mill	P/E	Price/ Sales	Price/ BV	$/bbl of prod- uction	Cents/ bbl reser- ves	Return 7/95- 7/96
Oil/Gas							
Chernogorneft	187	12.49	1.17	0.25	3.8	7.2	7%
Kominefl	135	-7.12	0.43	0.23	3.7	6.2	-41%
Kondpetroleum	86	-0.78	0.21	0.13	1.8	1.4	-29%
LUKoil	2948	14.5	0.88	1.3	8.4	26.7	41%
Megionneftegaz	185	4.17	0.58	0.15	1.9	7.7	71%
Nizhnevartovsk-neftegaz	136	-1.08	0.17	0.45	0.7	1.5	-43%
Noyabrskneftegaz	392	16.86	0.32	0.08	2.3	7.7	-18%
Orenburgneft	131	26.35	0.49	0.12	2.4	5.9	27%
Purneftegaz	264	20.04	0.95	0.46	3.8	4.9	-37%
Samaraneftegaz	186	36.4	0.58	0.35	2.9	9.1	-9%
Surgutneftegaz	703	4.74	0.58	0.26	2.8	6.5	74%
Tatneft	232	0.53	0.12	0.3	1.4	4.1	145%
Tomskneft	153	13.67	0.41	0.07	1.7	4.3	-5%
Yuganskneftegaz	534	61.2	0.87	0.45	2.8	5	-32%
Utility					$/MW installed ('000 $)		
Irkutskenergo	197	4.26	0.53	0.09	15.1		59%
Krasnoyarskenergo	59	0.71	0.18	0.16	7.22		111%
Lenenergo	97	9.75	0.24	0.32	19.3		159%

Mosenergo	717	1.88	0.39	0.64	49.6		147%
Samarenergo	81	2.07	0.14	0.12	23.1		53%
Sverdlovenergo	61	0.87	0.1	0.25	7.03		96%
UES	1078	2.53	11.2	1.56	0.06		103%
Telecom						**$/Access Line**	
Kubanelectrosviaz	70	4.22	1	0.45	132		17%
MGTS	300	10.5	1.39	0.38	80		62%
Nizhny NovgorodSviazinform	78	5.56	1.39	2.24	154		56%
Samrassviasinform	31	3.9	0.6	0.9	76		30%
StPetersburg Public Network	210	14.99	3.13	1.52	124		25%

Table 9.1. Fundamental data 1995

Company	Mkt cap in $ mill	P/E	Price/ Sales	Price/ BV	$/bbl of produc- tion	Cents/ bbl reserves	Return 7/96 -7/97
Oil/Gas							
LUKoil	6735	12.8	1.21	0.94	15.9	47	101%
Surgutneftegas	2090	2.6	0.66	0.33	8.6	19.2	187%
Yuganskneftegas	428	4.1	0.19	0.16	2.2	3.5	246%
Samarneftegas	145	1.6	0.25	0.21	2.2	6.9	246%
Noyabrskneftegas	452	10	0.24	0.16	3	9.1	152%
Megionneftegas	472	3.9	0.57	0.47	5	20	186%
Nizhnevartovsk-Neftegas	114	-4.7	0.07	0.04	0.74	1.3	486%
Chernogorneft	216	7.9	0.53	0.42	4.8	8.2	17%
Varyeganneftegas	60	-2	0.36	0.09	3.6	1.3	145%
Kondpetroleum	85	-1.2	0.2	0.07	2.3	1.4	183%
Udmurneft	93	0.9	0.21	0.16	2.1	4.4	385%
Tomskneft	203	2.5	0.28	0.11	2.5	6.2	326%
Komineft	88	-3.3	0.2	0.06	2.7	4	329%
Purneftegas	256	5.3	0.46	0.26	4.2	5.3	199%
Tatneft	651	1.8	0.29	0.28	3.6	12.5	158%

Utility				$/MW installed '000 $	
UES(level 3 consolid.)	3385	1.1	0.13	0.09	34	499%
Mosenergo	2483	4.6	0.82	0.73	172	108%
Irkutskenergo	512	7.9	1.05	0.29	39	231%
Lenenergo	390	45.4	0.52	0.49	73	328%
Bashkirnergo	180	2.7	0.19	0.21	35.4	482%
Samarenergo	153	2.4	0.18	0.29	44	238%
Sverdlovenergo	143	0.8	0.11	0.19	17.1	640%
Krasnoyarsk-Energo	117	1.5	0.2	0.12	22.9	290%
Permenergo	79	0.7	0.08	0.14	38	582%
Nizhnovenergo	34	0.9	0.06	0.09	23.9	967%
Telecom				$/Access line	
Rostelekom	2386	9.7	1.34	1.02		
MGTS	664	18.3	2.38	1.05	170	581%
PTS	319	9.6	2.83	0.91	182	408%
Perm Uralsviazinform	164	11.5	2.07	1.84	498	384%
Niz Novgorod-Sviazinform	117	4.3	1.59	1.08	230	531%
Kubanelectrosviaz	106	5.3	1.04	0.72	199	516%
Samara Sviazinform	48	3	0.68	0.53	116	1085%
Irkutsk Elektrosviaz	34	5.7	0.56	0.46	129	698%

Source: Brunswick Brokerage, market capitalization as of Nov. 3, 1995 and Brunswick Brokerage, market capitalization as of Sep. 6, 1996.

IX.A.3. Western Auditor, ADR, and Market Capitalization (WAM) – Dynamic measures of early market segmentation

The three factors composing the WAM score allow for an analysis of dynamic market segmentation and its effects on security pricing. While the subject of market segmentation is often referred to in the context of cost of capital of firms, the linkage between capital raising efforts and portfolio investors can easily be established.[4] In our context, the meaning of market segmentation is derived from firms possessing special characteristics that allow their equity to compete for international portfolio investment allocations. Hence, segmentation prevails when specific characteristics such as those depicted in diagram 9.1. prohibit foreign investors (or in some cases specific and large segments of foreign investors) from purchasing securities.

While the factors of Western auditors and the issuance of depository receipts are characteristics that are often within management's reach, market capitalization (which serves in the absence of reliable free float numbers as the best proxy for liquidity) seems to be less comparable to the other two market segmentation factors. Nevertheless, liquidity is a de facto criterion which can exclude a large segment of investors. Furthermore, as the origins of the Brazilian equity market have proven, liquidity is a factor which can also fall in the 'skill-will' matrix of management. The example of the Brazilian market during the early 1970s has shown that government policies can stimulate higher free float by giving tax incentives to companies with free float above 30%. This finally led to a larger number of companies having a more diversified shareholder base and higher free floats.[5] Moreover, in Russia it is often a function of the government's willingness to sell its stakes in many companies - an action which automatically would enhance liquidity.

---

[4] A good paper on market segmentation as a result of share ownership restrictions in Mexico is the following: Ian Domowitz, Jack Glen, and Anath Madhavan, "Market Segmentation and Stock Prices: Evidence from an Emerging Market." *Journal of Finance*, vol. 52 , no 3 (July 1997): 1059-1085.

[5] V.H. Errunza, "Efficiency and the Brazilian Capital Market, " *Journal of Banking and Finance*, 3 (1979): 355-382.

Diagram 9.1.   WAM factors of market segmentation

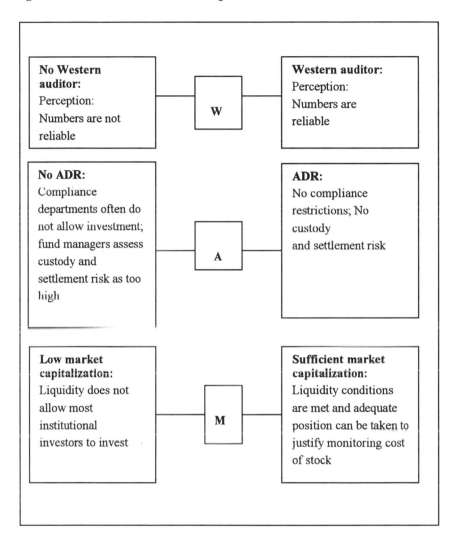

The following three charts display the WAM factor which is used to measure the security's attractiveness in terms of transparency, investability and liquidity. The three measures of Western auditor, depository receipt programs (ADRs), and market capitalization are used to proxy a score representing transparency and liquidity of the security. The aggregate WAM score is computed as the arithmetic average of the individual W-A-M scores for each security as shown in table 9.2.

Table 9.2.   WAM computation

CHARACTERISTIC/ SCORE	1	2	3
Western Auditor	No Western Auditor	Western Audit Planned	Existing Western Auditor
ADR Program	No ADR Program	ADR Program Planned	Existing ADR Program
Market Capitalization	Bottom 25% in Sector	Mid-50% in Sector	Top 25% in Sector

Chart 9.1. WAM factor oil/gas 95-96

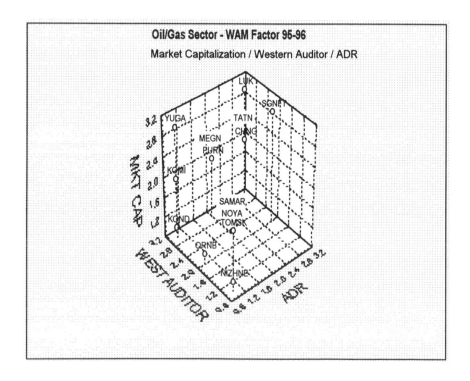

Chart 9.2. WAM factor utilities 95-96

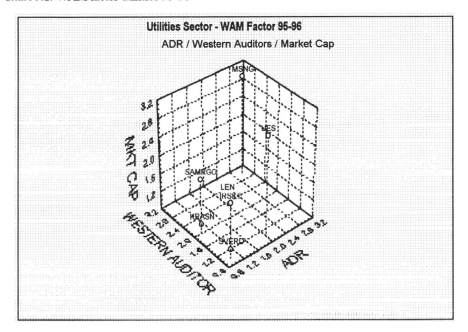

Chart 9.3. WAM factor telecoms 95-96

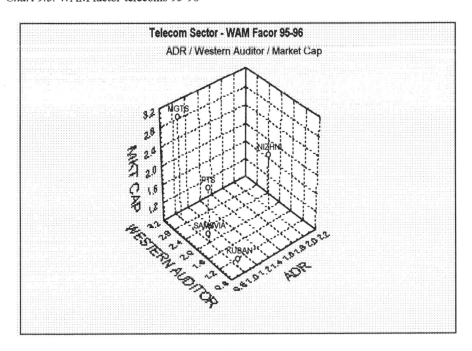

The same method of WAM illustration has been applied for the period from mid-96 to mid-97. The following three charts display the WAM results for the later period.[6]

Chart 9.4. WAM factor oil/gas 96-97

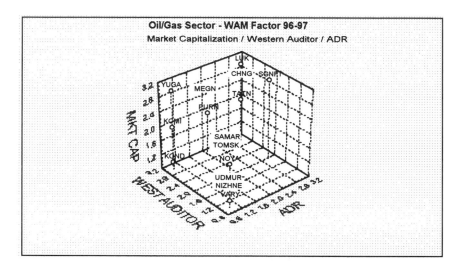

Chart 9.5. WAM factor telecom 96-97

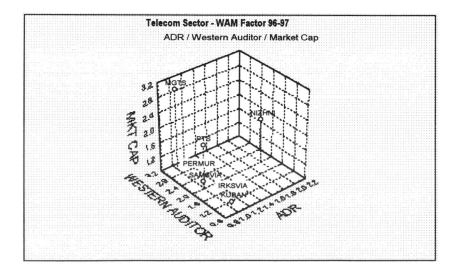

[6] The reason why market capitalization was used for both periods instead of free float is the result of free float data being less precise and therefore not an adequate tool for statistical analysis. Moreover, liquidity is fairly well approximated by market capitalization.

Chart 9.6. WAM factor utilities 96-97

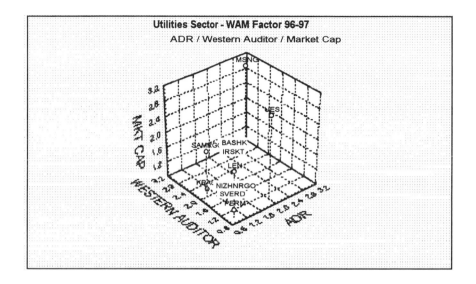

IX.A.4. Methodology

In order to determine which factors are most relevant for predicting securities' price performance, each security has been ranked by each individual fundamental ratio according to attractiveness versus its peers during the same time period. Intra-sector rankings have been applied, as different sectors mostly differ in their valuation ratios for basic economic reasons.

For example, a low price/sales ratio received a higher ranking than a high price/sales ratio, a low price/earnings ratio received a higher ranking than a high price/earnings ratio. The same concept is applied to asset-based ratios such as market capitalization/reserves, where the lower market capitalization/reserves ratio receives the higher ranking, etc.[7] Hence, the concept is simply based on the valuation of securities according to the various criteria. The underlying logic is that - ceteris paribus - assets should become fairly valued over time, which would imply that they sell at similar price/asset and price/financials ratios within each industry.

---

[7] The higher/lower ratios have been assigned in order to later compute the Spearman rank correlation coefficient with returns.

One may argue that there are other fundamental criteria at play which demand deep discounts or steep premia for specific securities. This is certainly true, but for the purposes of a pre-screening tool, which intends to recommend a specific group of favorably scoring securities   for further analysis, it is not relevant as it will be discovered at a later point. Furthermore, the scarcity of information on Russian equities, or other frontier market equities during the initial stages of the equity market   does not provide much additional information to most investors.

The same scoring method is applied to the WAM factor, where a lower WAM factor would receive a lower ranking, reflecting the underlying logic that less transparent and less liquid assets appear less favorably in the investment universe.   Finally, the returns for period 1 (mid-95 to mid-96) and for period 2 (mid-96 to mid-97) are ranked.   Higher returns would receive a higher ranking.   After completion of the ranking exercise, a correlation test can be conducted within each sector and time period between the fundamental variables' ranks and the return ranks, and between the WAM factor ranks and the return ranks.

The methodology used to establish statistical significance is Spearman's rank correlation coefficient. Spearman's rho is very similar to the ordinary correlation coefficient with one of the exceptions being that ranks are used as opposed to ordinary numbers.[8] Spearman's rho, as a non-parametric test which can be adjusted to observations under 20 ($n<20$), lends itself well to this exercise.

The computation formula is defined as follows:

(1)

$$\bar{r}_s = 1 - \frac{\sum d^2}{(\frac{1}{6})[n(n^2 - 1)] + 1}$$

where d is calculated as follows: assume x is the rank of security i according to criterion X, and y is the rank of the same security according to criterion Y. Then d can be defined as $d = y\text{-}x$. The number of observations is defined by

---

[8] Damodar N. Gujarati, *Basic Econometrics,* 3rd ed. (New York, NY: McGraw-Hill, 1995), 372.

n. Accordingly, the computation involves the essential step of measuring the differences of the ranks for each security under both criteria. For example, suppose one company with a very low P/E receives a P/E rank of 10 (which would be one of the highest). Further assume that the return of the same security is the highest in its industry group during the 12 months period following the initial availability of accounting data for a specific year and the ranking would be accordingly high (around 10). Then the measured difference in ranks would be small. The numerator in the formula defined above, which sums up the squared rank differences, would be small as well. Since the product of the division by a function of the sample size would subsequently be deducted from 1, such a scenario would, as expected, result in a high correlation coefficient.

To test for the statistical significance of Spearman's rho, the following t-test is used:

(2)

$$ t = \frac{r_s \sqrt{n-2}}{\sqrt{1-r^2}}, $$

with $\delta = n-2$ and the upper critical value of t for $\alpha=0.05$

IX.A.5. Results

The results for the Spearman's rho analysis can be found in table 9.3., where the Spearman correlation coefficient, the test statistic, and the significance level (under $\alpha=0.05$) are depicted.

Table 9.3. Spearman's rho analysis results (bolded* t-test are statistically significant)

PERIOD 1 "Genesis" (mid-1995 to mid-1996)

Oil/Gas 95-96	mkt cap	P/E	P/Sales	P/BV	$/bbl of production	cents/ bbl re- serves	WAM
Spearman's rho	0.316	0.873	-0.057	0.162	0.083	-0.364	0.555
t-test	1.153	**6.195***	-0.198	0.570	0.290	-1.354	**2.310***
Significance level	2.179	2.179	2.179	2.179	2.179	2.179	2.179

Utility 95-96	mkt cap	P/E	P/Sales	P/BV	$/MW installed '000 $	WAM
Spearman's rho	0.158	-0.053	-0.193	-0.614	-0.123	0.272
t-test	0.358	-0.118	-0.440	-1.740	-0.277	0.632
Significance Level	2.571	2.571	2.571	2.571	2.571	2.571

Telecom 95-96	mkt cap	P/E	P/Sales	P/BV	$/Access lines	WAM
Spearman's rho	0.238	-0.143	-0.048	0.143	-0.143	0.905
t-test	0.425	-0.250	-0.083	0.250	-0.250	**3.679***
Significance Level	3.182	3.182	3.182	3.182	3.182	3.182

PERIOD 2 "Wake-up phase" (mid-1996 to mid-1997)

Oil/Gas 96-97	mkt cap	P/E	P/Sales	P/BV	$/bbl of production	cents/bbl reserves	WAM
Spearman's rho	-0.162	-0.123	0.480	0.522	0.426	0.348	-0.212
t-test	-0.593	-0.447	1.970	**2.208***	1.698	1.337	-0.783
Significance Level	2.160	2.160	2.160	2.160	2.160	2.160	2.160

Utility 96-97	mkt cap	P/E	P/Sales	P/BV	$/MW installed '000 s	WAM
Spearman's rho	-0.566	0.759	0.892	0.711	0.388	-0.651
t-test	-1.943	**3.298***	**5.568***	**2.859***	1.192	**-2.423***
Significance Level	2.306	2.306	2.306	2.306	2.306	2.306

Telecom 96-97	mkt cap	P/E	P/Sales	P/BV	$/Access lines	WAM
Spearman's rho	-0.509	0.474	0.649	0.684	0.860	-0.018
t-test	-1.321	1.203	1.908	2.098	**3.763***	-0.039
Significance Level	2.571	2.571	2.571	2.571	2.571	2.571

The results of table 9.3. allow for formulation of the following conclusions:

1. The WAM factor is more important than fundamental valuation during the initial phase of the Russian equity market. The WAM factor is significant in the oil/gas sector and the telecom sector for period 1. During the first phase of the market development, none of the fundamental ratios are significant except for price/earnings in the oil and gas sector.[9]

2. Fundamental valuation becomes significant in the follow-up period when more research is at hand and investors are looking at companies more thoroughly. This is the time when the strict flow-of-funds type analysis subsides to an increasingly value-based analysis. During this period, fundamental ratios are significant in all sectors. Market capitalization/access lines is significant in the telecommunications industry (price/sales and price/book value are only "marginally" non-significant).[10] Price/book value is significant in oil/gas, while price/sales and market capitalization/bbl of production are missing the significance level by only a small margin (compared to period 1, where both measures do not come close to the significance level). In utilities, price/earnings, price/book value, and price/sales are all significant ratios for predicting returns for the next 12 months.

3. The WAM factor ceases to be significant during period 2. The exception is the utilities sector where the WAM factor takes on a negatively significant value. This implies that during period 2, investors are looking aggressively for undervalued securities on fundamental measures (see significance of fundamental ratios), and securities with low WAM scores. This means that investors are moving down the liquidity-transparency spectrum in search of more undervalued utilities. In fact, this development was supported by brokerages aggressively pitching the 'regional energos' or those utilities that are less known and located in one of the many regions of Russia.

---

[9] The P/E in the oil/gas sector during period 1 may in reality be less significant than it appears as the ranking procedure of the P/E had to make a relatively arbitrary judgement of whether the highest P/E or a very low, but negative, P/E, would take a lower rank. Finally the decision was made that a low, but negative P/E is less attractive than a very high, but positive P/E. The investor may have assessed the situation differently as a low, but negative P/E may foreshadow a turnaround, and a high P/E simply an expensive and over-valued stock.

[10] In strictly statistical terms this is, of course, not a correct formulation as "marginally" significant does not exist.

At this point it must also be noted that this life-cycle of securities valuation in pre-emerging markets can be interrupted by external shocks (such as the Asian crisis or an event such as Russia's currency devaluation in 1998). In such a situation, a flight to quality is likely to take place, and second and third tier stock selection is postponed to a later date. The initial concept regains the upper-hand and high WAM scores serve again as a good indicator of future performance.[11] The transition from stage 1 to stage 2 is crucial for the timing of investment decisions and the best indicator of timing is a large amount of research being dedicated to second and third tier stocks.

Diagram 9.2. Dynamic early valuation life-cycle of a frontier market

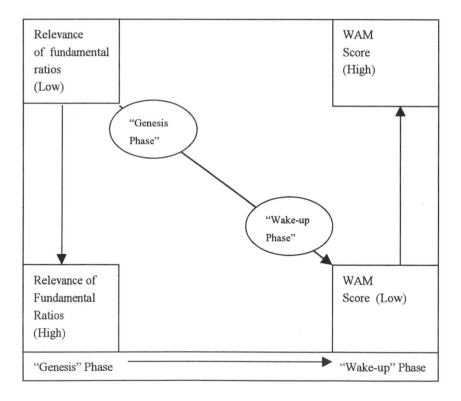

Diagram 9.2. graphically illustrates the results of the above described analysis and incorporates them into a general framework. The model describes the changing relevance of fundamental ratios and the WAM factor. The WAM score initially suggests strong relevance for predicting securities'

---

[11] Appendix II to chapter 9 illustrates the outperformance of Russian blue-chips (those with high WAM scores) during the recovery rally between December 1998 and March 1999.

returns and later again, becomes relevant as its negative score seems to filter securities that are on the 'value-chasing horizon' of investors moving down the liquidity-transparency spectrum in search of undiscovered value in frontier equity markets. Fundamental ratios rise to relevance as soon as solely WAM-initiated investments have been explored and more research enters the stage helping to educate investors about individual securities beyond their WAM characteristics.

IX.B. Screening framework for pre-emerging market securities valuation

IX.B.1. Four 'top-down' layers and one double-shelled nucleus of analysis

The previous section gave some evidence of the changing nature of valuation measures during the early phases of a frontier emerging equity market. This section will try to round up the discussion on valuation of pre-emerging market equities by building on the previous section and at the same time creating a larger framework for the valuation of pre-emerging equity markets throughout the early life-cycle.

While it is helpful to understand the dynamics of WAM valuation and fundamental valuation, and while it is important to appropriately use the WAM or the fundamental set of valuation criteria when the decision to enter a particular frontier emerging market has been made, it is at least as important to monitor some key indicators that allow the analyst to arrive at more general allocation decisions. In some cases this means that security-level analysis should be completely superseded by 'top-down' factors.[12]

In the case of pre-emerging markets, top-down analysis should always precede bottom-up analysis as overall market corrections mostly affect all stocks in thinly capitalized markets which are prone to quick capital withdrawal.[13] The common lack of a strong domestic investor base and the

---

[12] Macroeconomic/political factors and market valuation are commonly referred to as 'top-down' factors, whereas 'bottom-up' factors relate to the company level, or micro-analysis.

[13] It has been repeatedly established in securities market research that country allocation in emerging markets (not only frontier emerging markets) is the single most important decision. Studies showed that a portfolio of the worst performing securities in the best performing market often outperforms a portfolio of the best performing securities in the worst performing market.

relatively small number of dedicated country funds is usually not sufficient to provide a stabilizing momentum and resilience in case of top-down pessimism. Thus, during an unfavorable top-down outlook, international investors can chose to completely ignore the market and re-allocate investments to other markets.[14]

From this follows that the above mentioned WAM/fundamental criteria analysis merely forms the nucleus of pre-emerging equity market analysis. Around this nucleus, we can establish at least three layers of analysis. The first layer is political risk. This is a topic which generally is discussed at length in non-financial publications. At this point it would explode the frame of this book to engage in a detailed discussion of political risk analysis in frontier emerging markets. There are a number of basic guidelines that should be followed, and those are depicted in table 9.4.

IX.B.2.   Political risk check list

Among the many political risk indicators it is reasonable to single out the following: The composition of parliament and the reliance on one leading political figure is well demonstrated in the case of Romania and the Czech Republic during 1997, where parliament was split over economic reform and the minority coalition partner or the opposition would not forgo any opportunity to discredit the ruling faction. Such a situation often occurs in newly democratic countries where no single party can win majority support during the elections and consequently must rely on compromise partnerships, often with less desirable and less reform-minded political entities. A weak coalition government also makes the country's economic policy vulnerable to policy populism which rarely serves in the best interest of public fiscal and monetary management.

The threat of military coups or fundamentalists harassing foreigners and the civilian population, is higher in countries, such as Turkey and Algeria, where secularism has not ended the battle against religious hard-liners, which more often than not, have a manifest interest in preserving the status quo or regressing to undemocratic or vulgarly populist concepts. Necessary and revenue-creating privatization and deregulation are often sacrificed on the altar of political appeasement with such forces.

---

[14] The Czech Republic comes to mind, when during 1997 because of the negative overall outlook, most investors completely avoided exposure to this market. The case of Romania during 1998/1999 presents a more fitting example in the frontier market context.

A rise in unemployment and wage arrears can culminate in civil unrest. Ukraine has had its share of miner strikes over the past two years, and so may Russia if public wages remain unpaid. This type of 'wage-arrears-budget-deficit-financing' which takes credit from public employees, is not uncommon in transitional economies that are adhering to IMF/World Bank austerity programs, and which, among other things, require low inflation and low budget deficits. Extended public credit-creation by means of building up wage arrears can be a destabilizing factor, particularly if workers simply do not have alternative income sources.

Nepotism and crony-capitalism exist in virtually every country. Cases such as Indonesia or Nigeria, where tremendous amounts of public funds are channelled into economic value-destroying firms, have proven disastrous. A good indicator is to frequently monitor the extent to which the financial system fulfills its role as an intermediator of capital. If loans are given on the basis of names as opposed to creditworthiness, a red flag should be raised. The absence or inadequacy of bankruptcy laws often contributes to the opaque nature of the real economic and financial status of companies and their creditors.

Corruption and crime may affect the transparency of the companies listed on the stock exchange. Investors should be aware that company property and funds may be diverted into bribery fees and security payments. Most emerging market firms are not bound by the Foreign Corrupt Practices Act, which prohibits US firms from paying bribes, mainly for shareholder value protection. In addition to robbing potential dividend payments from the shareholders, corruption and crime cast a dark shadow over the securities market infrastructure as a whole, which can affect overall valuation.

In practical terms, a lack of legal recourse can be a serious problem. While most nations will give evidence of some type of legal recourse, in practice the cost and chance of success will outweigh the possible benefit of taking legal action. This can affect minority shareholder rights and any type of contractual agreements that have been signed and have not been abided by.

Unresolved supraregional and interregional conflicts, such as Chechnya, Taiwan, the Ukrainian submarine port of Sevastopol, Kosovo, or the PKK in Turkey, etc. can at any time take on the center stage of news. While they often may have a marginal immediate effect on the market, the sheer complexity, as they are often ill-defined by mainstream journalists, and scope of such conflicts can create devastating consequences. Pipelinecracking terrorism in the Caspian region, and cut-offs of gas supply to Ukraine by Russia are just two to be mentioned. It is a quintessential task for the astute pre-emerging market analyst to keep abreast of such developments. There are several regional reports issued on a weekly basis, and many more web sites that cover local tensions beyond CNN headline material. Most of them are helpful, accessible, and inexpensive.[15]

Finally, the popularity and sustainability of current reforms are as important a checkpoint as all others. Reforms, which are not backed by the population, are to die at a young age. Romania is the best example at hand. It has been almost eight years that reformers have struggled simply to be defeated by reactionary forces in the political spectrum, which exploited any form of hardship programs as a fertile ground to launch a populist campaign, eventually slowing down economic reform.

Table 9.4.   Political risk checkpoints for pre-emerging markets

Political risk check list	*Case examples*
Composition of parliament? Reliance on one leader?	Romania, Czech Rep.
Strength of military / Fundamentalists? Possibility of coup?	Turkey, Algeria, Paraguay
Rise in unemployment/Wage arrears/Civil unrest?	Russia, Ukraine
Nepotism-and crony-capitalism-based trade regime?	Indonesia
Corruption/crime?	Nigeria, Slovakia, S. Afri.
No legal recourse?	Nigeria, Slovakia
Latent and unresolved supraregional conflicts?	Russia (Chechnya), China (Taiwan)
Popularity and sustainability of reforms?	Romania, Turkey

IX.B.3.   Macro screening tool

The second layer of analysis is the overall macro-situation of the country. Again a topic which could fill volumes and which still would fall short of completeness. The engaged pre-emerging markets analyst who cannot dedicate all efforts to macro-analysis is advised – as a sanity check on any

[15] Particularly useful are reports emanating from the New York-based East-West Institute which e-mails regional reports to subscribers.

other analysis- to use the Eurobond-US-Treasury spread as a proxy for the macro-outlook of the country. While fixed income default risk is not necessarily a substitute for more comprehensive analysis, and while the willingness and ability to service and repay sovereign debt is not necessarily the most conclusive indicator of macro-economic risks affecting the equity market, the rudimentary stages of pre-emerging equity market index performance have revealed a strong negative correlation with the sovereign spread developments (see chart 9.7.).

This leads to the obvious conclusion that frontier equity market rallies are mostly a function of the declining risk premium of the country. To illustrate the theoretical relationship between the risk free rate and the value of an equity, the following excursion will be taken.

IX.B.3.1. Equity valuation and the risk free rate – crucial nexus in frontier emerging markets – theoretical underpinnings

The theoretical basis for such risk-reduction-based rallies can be illustrated in simplified terms with the following formula derived from Gordon's Growth Model.[16]

Gordon's growth model:

(3) $P = DPS_1/r - g$

where:

P = price per share

DPS_1 = *expected dividend per share in year 1;*

R= *required rate of return on equity – discount rate*

G= *growth rate in dividends.*

Expected dividend in year 1 using year 0's dividend (DPS_0):

---

[16] For a detailed discussion of this technique please refer to *Investment Valuation* by Aswath Damodaran.

(4) $DPS_0 = EPS_0$ x payout ratio

     $EPS_0 =$ *current year (year 0) earnings per share*

Thus, year 1 dividend can be computed as:

(5) $DPS_1 = EPS_0$ x payout ratio x $(1+g)$.

Accordingly, equation (3) can be transformed as follows:

(6) $P = EPS_0$ x payout ratio x $(1+g)/(r-g)$.

Current ROE_0 can be defined as:

(7) $ROE_0 = EPS_0 / BV_0$ or $EPS_0 = ROE_0$ x BV_0

where $BV_0 =$ *current book value per share*

Substituting EPS in equation (6) with equation (7), results in:

(8) $P = ROE_0$ x BV_0 x payout ratio x $(1+g) / (r-g)$.

To replace current (ROE_o) with (ROE_1) based on expected earnings, equation

(8) can be restated as follows:

(9) $PBR_0 = ROE_1$ x payout ratio $/ (r-g)$

This can be further simplified by relating ROE to the growth rate:

(10) $g = ROE$ x $(1-$ payout ratio$)$

which can be restated as:

(11) Payout ratio $= 1-g /ROE$,

and payout ratio in equation (9) can be substituted with equation (11).

(12) $PBR_0 = ROE_1$ x $(1-g /ROE) / (r-g)$

This can be further simplified to:

(13) $PBR_0 = (ROE_1 - g) / (r-g)$

The three main assumptions required for Gordon's growth model are (1) estimation of a sustainable ROE, (2) estimation of a sustainable growth rate, and (3) the cost of equity.

Sustainable ROE

The best method of deriving a sustainable ROE for a frontier emerging market company is generally to average various forecasts from sell-side analysts and the company's own guidance. There is little use in creating a new model for a frontier emerging market company in order to compute a proprietary number for the sustainable ROE. While a sustainable ROE derived from a diligently created model may be superior to brokers' estimates, the time horizon of most frontier emerging market investors will not allow reality to reassert itself. Thus, current sell-side research analysts' estimates are most likely the estimates which will be used by most other buy-side analysts in order to make investment decisions. The critical reader may disagree with this notion. However, a valuation dimension based on lateral thinking is superior in a time context when prices will move *before long-run reality will have a chance to reassert itself.* At this point, it must be emphasized that the main purpose of this discussion is to achieve superior investment performance, not to derive the absolute real value of an asset.

Frequently, sell-side research analysts will not provide sustainable ROEs but only ROEs for specific years. In such cases, a cumulatively aggregated ROE should be computed.

Sustainable ROE = f ($\varnothing$ sell-side research analysts' sustainable ROE, company's guidance)

Sustainable growth rate:

The sustainable growth rate on the other hand is to be derived from a set of variables mostly not available in research reports. In mature markets the sustainable growth rate would be a function of the sustainable competitive advantage period and the GDP growth rate. In frontier emerging equity markets, the sustainable growth rate is mostly a function of the GDP growth rate.

Required rate of return – discount rate: CAPM= Rf + beta (Rp)

where:

Rf = *risk free rate = the long bond of the local market or the Eurobond spread over US-treasuries added to the US long bond.*

Beta = *industry beta (in emerging markets this is often a very imprecise measure for reasons related to non-stationarity of betas and market segmentation theory)*

Rp = *equity risk premium (a function of the equity market infrastructure and historical relationship between equities and fixed income; in mature markets the equity risk premium is normally assessed to be between 2.5% and 3.5%. In frontier markets the equity risk premium should be in the range between 4% and 7%.*

A more scientific approach to the equity risk premium would be to use the US equity risk premium (as a valuation benchmark for global securities) and to adjust it for the higher volatility of the emerging market in the most recent time period. This could then be computed as the standard deviation of the frontier equity market divided by the standard deviation of the US equity market. Rp = annualized standard devation S&P500 / annualized standard deviation Frontier Equity Market Index.

However, using this approach one finds a fundamental problem. The volatility measure of the Frontier Equity Market Index is already implied in the sovereign bond spread number. To use both measures would lead to the double-counting of risk. In order to adjust for this mistake, one can compute the correlation between dollar returns of equities in the Frontier Equity Market and sovereign bonds [double-counting adjustment correlation factor (DCACORRF)]. The correlation coefficient could then be used to adjust for the equity risk premium.

Rp = *(annualized standard deviation S&P500 / annualized standard deviation Frontier Equity Market Index)*(1-DCACORRF)*

The risk free rate is the crucial ingredient in the above described valuation formula. The sensitivities to the risk free rate (Rf) can be illustrated in table 9.5. The assumptions are a sustainable growth rate of 3%, sustainable ROE of 10%, equity risk premium of 5%, beta=1, and the risk free rate (Rf) of 5% for scenario A and 10% for scenario B.

Example of valuation sensitivity of risk free rates in frontier equity markets:

r = Rf + beta* Rp

| Scenario A | r =5%+(1 x 5%)=10% |
| Scenario B | r =10%+(1 x 5%)=15% |

The computation of target Price/Book value (P/B) follows:

$PBR_0 = (ROE_1 - g) / (r-g)$

Table 9.5. Sensitivity of valuation to risk free rate

	Rf (A) = 5%	Rf (B)=10%
Target P/B	1x	0.58x

As we can see, the fair value of the security is determined to be 1x its book value under a risk free rate of 5% and only 0.58x its book value under a risk free rate of 10%. This clears the understanding of why we can observe the relationship depicted in chart 9.7. below.

Chart 9.7. Russian index and Russian Eurobond spreads over US treasuries (bps) 1996-1998

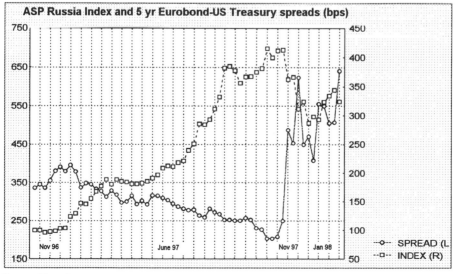

Source: Bloomberg

Naturally, Eurobond-spreads cannot substitute for a more formal approach to macro-analysis, which would have to include public finances, economic growth, inflation, interest rates, privatization, debt burden, deregulation and all matters pertaining to the viability and sustainability of the currency regime. However, for the purpose of this chapter which provides pre-screening tools, the use of Eurobond-spreads as a proxy variable for macro-economic outlook is helpful.[17] The continuous assessment of the macro-economic outlook, which is captured in just one number, can be a highly effective tool to make cross-pre-emerging market comparisons. Furthermore, the fixed income yield can also be used to assess the attractiveness of competing investment alternatives (such as equity vs bonds). Turkey has historically provided a striking example of this.

IX.B.4.   Equity infrastructure assessment

The third layer of analysis has already been discussed at the end of the chapter on equity market infrastructure. It revolves around the question of whether the equity market infrastructure improvement allows for the closing of valuation gaps with other markets. In Russia, the question has often arisen as to why the best Russian telecommunications companies still trade at a significant discount to comparable firms such as Telmex in Mexico. The answer is simply found in the second-rate nature of Russian equity market infrastructure.[18]

The re-rating process takes place when investors collectively agree that the trading system, settlement system, clearing house, custody, shareholder rights legislation, stock market supervision, etc. have improved and created a safer investment environment. Hence, continuously monitoring such developments, becomes as important a task for valuation as the top-down and the micro-valuation (WAM/fundamental) analysis.

---

[17] The Eurobond spread qualifies equally well for a 'rough' assessment of the political climate, as the ability and willingness to service and repay debt is also a function of the political situation in a country.

[18] For details on what implies second-rate equity market infrastructure, please refer to the chapter on the Russian equity market infrastructure and particularly the section where the valuation context is discussed.

IX.B.5.   Overview of screening framework

Diagram 9.3. illustrates the three main layers of pre-emerging market equity screening and the suggested time intervals in which a review appears adequate.[19] Furthermore, once the WAM/fundamental level of analysis has been reached, an even more precise tool, which suggests the timely switching from the primary usage of asset-based measures to the primary usage of financials-based measures, can enhance performance.[20]

Diagram 9.3.Three layers and a double nucleus of pre-emerging market equity screening

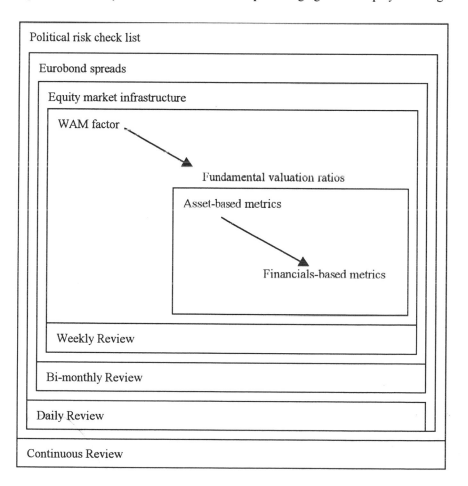

---

[19] For further reference on time-series/cross-sectional studies of political and economic risk variables and their impact on the predictability of valuations and future returns, see also: C. B. Erb; C.R. Harvey and T.E. Viskanta, "Political Risk, Economic Risk, and Financial Risk," *Financial Analysts Journal* (Nov/Dec 1996): 29-46.

[20] As indicated in discussion accompanying chart 9.0.

Appendix I to chapter IX.

Chart 9.0. Early life cycle of valuation – From asset-based to financials-based valuation

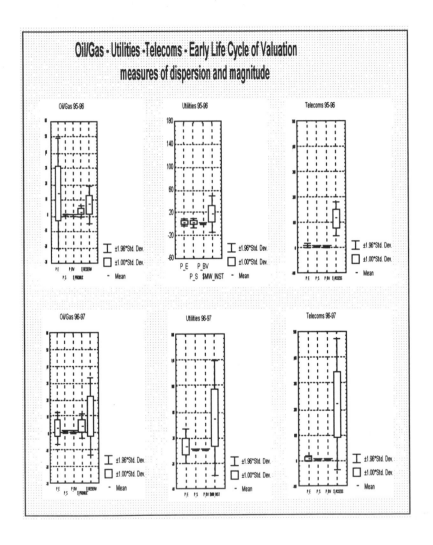

Appendix II to chapter IX.

Chart 9.8. Blue–chip underperformance and outperformance during times of foreign investment outflows and foreign investment recovery 'vulture' players – a proof of market segmentation theory

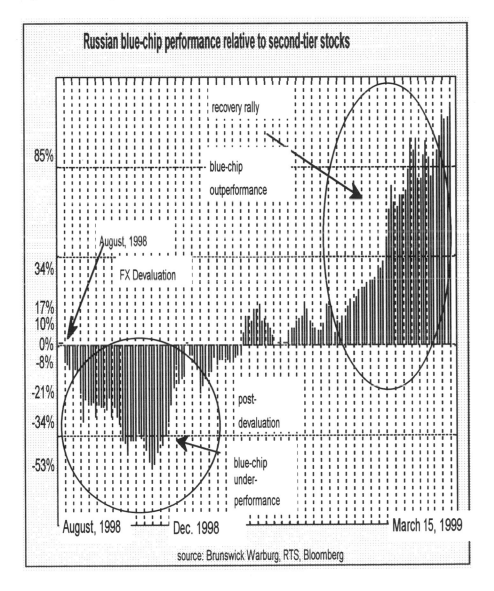

Chapter 10

The Philology of Frontier Equity Markets
Anatomy of the pre-emerging market valuation debate

The frequent absence of reliable data and the ubiquitous presence of ambiguous sources exposes frontier markets more to the perils of 'journalistic gossip' and complacent thinking than more mature equity markets. In many cases, the sources of opinion-molding statements and conclusions are not investment professionals, but the financial newswires and their following. To understand the relationship between stock market philology and stock market valuation, a short excursion into the anatomy of market opinion formation is useful.

X.A.   Anatomy of market opinion formation in frontier emerging markets

Financial markets are largely a mechanism where prices reflect information of tradable assets. The purpose is to establish a clearing price at which there will be equal demand from buyers and supply from sellers. Such a price can be defined as the equilibrium price. In the case of traded goods, and in a simplified world, the clearing price is established by sellers of goods and buyers of goods. In a simple case, the buyer has a need for the good, possibly as an input into a manufactured product, and the seller has empirical and current knowledge of the market for her goods. This means that the seller can gauge the demand to some degree. The price, which then will be a function of the production cost of the good, the required profit margin, and the relative scarcity premium or abundance discount, is most likely a fair one reflecting demand, supply and the real economic factors underlying the supply and demand schedules. The demand and supply curves are highly visible and the merchants experienced in their trade. On such premises, a distortion in prices would be highly unlikely.

Now let us visit the case of frontier equity markets. Firstly, the goods are no longer tangible but represent intangible claims on equity and their future stream of dividends. The companies, in some cases, are only officially represented by their paper claims. In reality, management in frontier markets often does not recognize portfolio investors as legitimate minority owners of their company, but rather views them as an intruding minority. Informational transparency is poor and often only available for the current time period. Historical data is rarely available to the degree appropriate to conduct Graham & Dodd-style investment analysis. The investor knows little about the company's products, services, competitive position and outlook within the economy. Most certainly, no reliable information on the industry and its competitive landscape exists. Regulatory structures for an industry, or monopoly term structures protecting local industries before foreign competition can enter the market (in the case of telecommunications companies or electric utilities) are a function of government regulatory actions and the most powerful lobby, which usually needs to be accommodated.

Hence, relying on industry regulations favoring particular investments often turns out to be a rather unprofitable way of conducting frontier emerging equity market investment analysis. There may be some research on the company – recently written by young frontier market Wall Street analysts or locally hired analysts who recently graduated from the local poly-technical institute and who fashion some English proficiency. In either case, the research quality will correspond to the experience of the analysts and the reliability of sources of information available. Initially, information will be of a highly qualitative nature and scarce in quantitative and objective parameters. This is a snapshot of the condition in a frontier market.

The frontier equity market can now be repositioned in the framework of price determination and supply and demand of goods and services. Investors buy with the expectation of future dividend streams resulting from the operations of a company. Dividends, in frontier markets, however, are not common. Most companies are cash-starved and need free cash flow for re-investment to maintain current operations, as opposed to growing operations. This offers the first deviation from the simplified market place described above. Investors in frontier markets are better described as the maintainers and builders of an economy of which they know little. Companies are, in most cases, far away from the growth stage. Production facilities or generation facilities and infrastructure still need to be built and maintained before earnings are recorded and customers are able to pay for companies' goods and services. In this sense, frontier market investors are deep value investors at the heart of the definition of value investment.

Apart from the inadequate visibility dimension at the micro-economic level, the macro-economic dimension offers an even greater challenge. The examples of Brazil in early 1999, Russia in 1998 or South-East Asia in late 1997 established an unparalleled proof of broker research, multilateral institutions, rating agencies and investors going in the wrong direction until the latent reality surfaced and the macro-economic variables reasserted themselves in the most forceful way. The lack of current visibility naturally implies that evidence of investment success, in most instances, will appear only in the distant future. The distant future will tell whether companies' products will be sold or services will be competitively offered. In the meantime, before the actual realization of financial results and the payment of dividends, the frontier market game is on. Little evidence suggests whether government economic plans are realistic and feasible, and there is little hard evidence about which companies will be successful. There are no track records. Investors have to map their own scenarios and outcomes by making many assumptions. It is at this point when a factor, which in the financial community has become known as 'sentiment', powerfully enters the stage of frontier market investing.

'Sentiment' has filled the explanatory void of market behavior which does not follow the rules of investment analysis. It is the irrational foresight investors seek in order to make investment decisions which can not be justified at the current time due to the absence of real tangible evidence and lack of data availability. For example, sentiment is mostly used as an explanation for undershooting and overshooting of asset prices. The reason why undershooting and overshooting exists is explained by anchoring theory and simple extrapolation of the past into the future.[1] If Indonesian asset prices declined 25% yesterday, the likelihood of them declining further is higher than the likelihood of a price reversal – an often observed form of temporary crisis autocorrelation. The question now becomes: when is the price decline enough to justify the new investment environment? Clearly, a new piece of information has to emerge in order to reverse 'sentiment' and cause prices to rebound.

It is at this point when trends are more powerful in forecasting future price direction than absolute analysis. The measuring of risk premia and economic forecasting is a highly imprecise science, therefore it is nearly impossible to find a target price for an equity market under a specific

---

[1] See chapter 2 for a more detailed explanation of "anchoring."

economic policy scenario implying a specific risk premium. This is especially true for frontier equity markets at extreme valuations.

Given the impotence of precise value derivation, a directional approach must be taken. This means that any frontier market which is moving into a favorable risk-premium direction, will benefit, and vice versa. A good example was the February 1999 rally in the Russian equity market which was solely based on the notion that the restructuring of GKOs would finally bring an end to the increasingly distracting uncertainty about the no-longer-tradable GKOs, and the hope that some of the money would eventually be forcefully channeled into the equity market.[2] This rally was purely based on trend dynamics. None of Russia's economic problems had been solved, and speculation was still open on how grave the real economic consequences of the 1998 devaluation would be. Yet, in the absence of real events and facts, directional trends can be enormously powerful drivers of share prices. The allusion to a restructuring of the GKO stock and the chance that some of the proceeds would find their way into the equity market was sufficient to turn the Russian equity market, which already had priced in total collapse.

Logically, it is true that indicators of trends causing a swing in market sentiment are the more powerful, the more extreme the valuation of the market is. In Russia, valuations had been at extreme 'blow-out' levels since the devaluation of the Russian Ruble in the fall of 1998. The possibility that the outstanding GKO restructuring would take place and be completed at one point did not create a more optimistic valuation for LUKoil, the Russian oil company. However, the completion of the GKO restructuring bundled with the vague notion of GKO proceeds flowing into the Russian equity market, helped the share price to recover by 40%.[3] This phenomenon can be explained with a theory referred to as the 'disjunction effect' which states that investors have a tendency to wait with a decision until some type of information is released – regardless of whether it is relevant or not.[4]

The November 1998 to spring 1999 Russian share prices rally was probably the best example of how important directional trends can be in frontier emerging markets. While it had become fashionable to ignore the Russian equity market since the currency devaluation, because the problems

---

[2] GKOs are local currency denominated government debt obligations, which had been 'frozen' by the government following the August 1998 devaluation of the Ruble. Many of the GKO debt holders were foreign investors. Credit Suisse First Boston and its clients accounted for the largest share of foreign-held GKO debt obligations.

[3] The LUKoil rally was later fueled by a rising oil price in Spring 1999.

[4] Please refer to chapter 2 for more information on the disjunction effect.

were so grave and the solutions remote and difficult to implement, the example of the early 1999 Russian rally showed that a new mindset is required in a frontier equity market situation at extreme valuations. It is at this point when analysis is best conducted through the lenses of the relativists and decision-making must shrewdly ignore the human boundaries of agency theory.[5]

The single most important notion in frontier emerging market equity investing is the fact that prices are determined by the 'debate'. The debate is the continuous interpretation of events pertaining to those factors which, in fundamental terms, should determine the fair value of equities. Of course, in the absence of reality checks and real and reliable information, the arguments building the 'debate' are the only true indicators of which the frontier emerging market portfolio manager should be keenly aware, and in which every market participant is a critical purveyor of information.

X.B.   Aristotle's Art of Persuasion applied to frontier market dynamics

One framework which lends itself particularly well to the illustration of securities price behavior in pre-emerging markets is a derivation of an argumentation by Aristotle used in his *Rhetoric*.[6] According to *Rhetoric* three main elements fuel the art of persuasion: *Logos, ethos, and pathos*. Logos stands for reason and rationale. Numbers and facts are the main drivers of *logos*. *Ethos* represents authority and scope. *Pathos* reflects emotion, passion, and instinctual behavior. In the case of frontier markets, logos, ethos and pathos are three dynamic elements which drive share price performance.

Diagram 10.0. illustrates the relationship between the three forces underlying the art of persuasion, or in our case, the frontier equity market valuation debate. Intelligently, Aristotle's work referred to *The Art of Persuasion*, rather than the art of *conviction*. In frontier markets there will always be sufficient margin for doubt and uncertainty to refrain from the notion of conviction. However, decisions are likely to be made on the basis of persuasion. Logos, the power of reason and facts, may find the frontier emerging market environment attractively valued, and find that the market reveals great potential. Even a scarce amount of data and information may lead to this recognition. Ethos, the purveyor of authority and scope – most

---

[5] See chapter 2 for details of the limitations imposed on traders by agency theory.
[6] Please refer also to Amelie Oksenberg Rorty, *Essays on Aristotle's Rhetoric* (1996).

likely represented by the brokerage community – will wake up to the faint notion of an attractively valued market as it has been established by logos.

Diagram 10.0. The art of persuasion in frontier equity markets

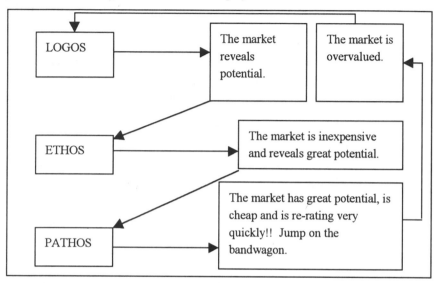

The agent of ethos will publish many research reports and gain the interest of investors in the frontier emerging market. The next step will be increased investment activity in this market. Most likely, small volumes are traded, mainly generated by true pioneer–type investors. In many cases, non-institutional, private or hedge fund assets will be the first to explore the market and drive up prices disproportionately to the underlying investment volumes. At this point, the still virtuous and rational cycle acquires the devious honor of admitting the force of pathos – emotion and competition – into its rows.

Pathos will ascertain that the share price movement is well documented and becomes the topic of conversation in the mainstream investment community. Many more investors will jump on the bandwagon and drive prices to even higher levels. At this point, investors have become oblivious to underlying fundamentals – particularly in light of the flabbergasting returns everyone is achieving. It is also at this point when the scarce information fueling the power of logos reaches a critical mass to reassert itself versus the strong valuation disequilibrium generated by the pathos/ethos-driven share price rally. Now the valuations are only insufficiently based on logos. Once this happens, and even the scarce data is sufficient to point out the out-of-line valuation, the forces of logos will correct the market – frequently this happens in a rather uncontrolled fashion. It is now obvious to mention that entering the frontier emerging equity market during the stage dominated by pathos, investment returns will most likely be negative.

Elaboration:

Ethos, logos and pathos translated into the context of frontier markets

Ethos:

Brokerage research reports are essential - the more, the better. The authority and influence exerted by a large global brokerage house on a frontier equity market cannot be overestimated. For example, if Merrill Lynch decides to publish a research report on a company with a price target substantially above the current trading price of a frontier equity market security, the company's share price is likely to benefit. The mechanism is similar to that when a major investigative broadcast program reports a special event. For example, the *60 Minutes* report on an event discovers that a specific development is crucial to the security of a nation. Most likely the topic will become the subject of conversation and further inquiry and consequent actions are likely. In this example, the producers of *60 Minutes* use their scope and authority to portray an event or disseminate an opinion. The same mechanism applies to frontier equity markets where information dissemination is less intense and the interpretation of events by a brokerage with scope and authority has a dramatic, and often amplifying effect on the market.

Logos:

In order for brokers to issue an opinion on a frontier market or a security traded in a frontier market environment, logos must be present. As logos stands for the facts and the numbers creating the basis for investment analysis, the agent of ethos cannot exist without logos nurturing its arguments and viewpoints. The question, however, remains as to what extent logos is needed, and how much it is used by the agent of ethos. In a developed and mature market, an abundance of information and facts usually exists. The art in such markets is to properly interpret such facts. For example, the semiconductor industry benefits from daily, or hourly flows of data. The research skill of the sell-side analysts in this industry must lie in interpreting and tying together all the facts, and in creating an overall sensible and realistic view of the future developments. Frontier market analysts do not have the luxury of information abundance, and are in the less enviable position of having to fill the gaps with sober and partially empirical and heuristic analysis. The precision of such analyses, of course, is often questionable and there is no short-term check on the interpretation of the detailed picture. At this point, the role of ethos is likely to levitate off the faint trails of logos (the factual information we have), and frontier markets can enter valuation spheres increasingly detached from underlying fundamentals.

Pathos:

Pathos stands for emotion and passion. In the context of frontier market analysis, pathos plays an important role. As illustrated in diagram 10.0., it is the accelerator which bypasses the forces of logos until an often critical point when valuation has moved so grossly away from an equilibrium, that even scarce information fueling logos may be sufficient to reassert itself, and reposition the equity market on more realistic valuations.

X.C.   Unweaving the frontier market debate with the theory of memes

To understand the three forces driving the debate in frontier market equity analysis, it appears reasonable to take a closer look at the substance forming a debate. Richard Dawkins refers to the theory of 'memes' in his famous book *The Selfish Gene* (1976). This theory describes that memes, similar to genes, are instructing replications. As opposed to genes, memes are transmitted from brain to brain, not from one cell to the next. Dawkins' gives the quite illustrative example about how certain tunes can 'infect' another person's brain and consequently make the person sing or whistle the melody against one's will. This is pure meme talk. Further, Dawkins states that memes are often not just a tune but an endlessly repeated phrase – sometimes even without any obvious significance or redeeming qualities. Memes, just like genes, survive better in the presence of specific other memes. Dawkins compares the 'cooperative cartels' of genes, which are formed by certain gene pools, to the cooperative cartel of memes – also called a memeplex. D.C. Dennett, author of 'Darwin's Dangerous Idea' (1995) , and 'Consciousness Explained' (1991), even goes a step further and defends the hypothesis that human consciousness is itself a huge complex of memes:

Memes, like genes, form complexes. For example, Silicon Valley is a potent meme bolstered by a complex including such terms as 'high-tech companies', 'venture capitalism' and 'young entrepreneurs'. Components of a meme, once introduced tend to be very robust to changes, and in many cases are ineradicable. The biggest question of memes is whether they selfishly replicate or they serve the purpose of 'Darwinian fitness.' While it is difficult to understand the redeeming qualities of brains being 'infected' by a tune, it is much easier to understand those memes which enable us to learn by imitation in order to conduct our lives more efficiently. The uncharted meme territory, however, is where a certain memeplex prepares us to be more or less receptive to new memes and hence to actions resulting from adopting new memes.

The example which immediately comes to mind is that of political ideology. A right-wing biased memeplex will make it more difficult to absorb information which carries 'unfitting' data with a left-wing bias. Therefore, memes may not always act on our behalf and in our best interest. The 'right-wing political' memeplex, which a person may have established, will not allow ideologically different memes to enter the brain as easily. In the end, this may be in every person's interest as it smoothes out variation and adds an element of stability to our thinking. Such a non-cooperative memeplex may shelter us from groups of information which we have established as non-desirable for the conduct of our life. In this sense it may be good to have a protective non-cooperative meme cartel in place. But at the same time, it must be recognized that with our more or less receptively inclined memeplexes in our brain, we are likely to react more slowly and need a critical mass of certain memes in order to include them into our larger pool of memes. The existence of a *critical mass* is especially important if new meme signals are not compatible with an existing memeplex. If we have memeplexes in place that are receptive to certain memes, such as Christians who believe in God (a very strong memeplex) and are likely to be receptive to the notion of 'resurrection' and 'forgiveness', the danger is that new memes are uncritically absorbed and thus lead to un-Darwinian behavior, which may not be optimal for our survival.

In the context of frontier emerging markets, complexes of memes are still in the process of being created. As a consequence of the relatively young age, memes have only created less robust complexes during the short frontier emerging market existence. Just like genes, complexes of memes can mutate. The case of Russia presents us with a timely example. While Russia was initially perceived as a gold mine for daring investors and later for the mainstream mutual funds, the frontier equity market of Russia has spoiled the meme of frontier emerging markets radically over the past two years.   Charts 10.0. and 10.1. quantitatively illustrate the development of memes in emerging markets.

As previously noted, memes replicate themselves, often only by simple repetition. This finally leads to humans adopting the meme and building memeplexes.   An interesting memeplex is emerging markets: 'growth,' 'high risk,' and 'high return investments'. This memeplex has mutated to a new one which could be composed of the following memes: 'currency devaluation,' 'contagion,' 'crisis,' 'losing money,' 'high risk,' and 'negative returns.'

Chart 10.0. Financial meme and its impact

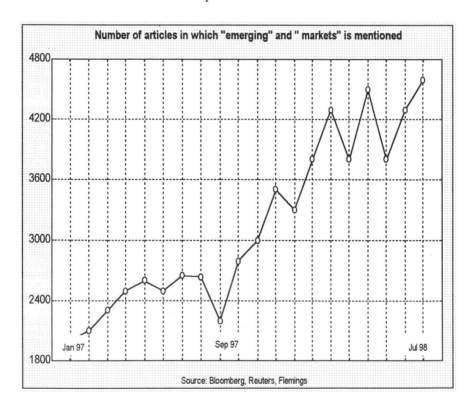

As memes can direct behavior of investors in frontier emerging markets, it becomes paramount for the skilful portfolio manager to relentlessly study the memetic evolution in the field of frontier emerging markets. Only then can opportunities and risks be detected by assessing the trends which may affect the memeplex, before the broad meme pool mutates.

Chart 10.1. Frontier emerging market memes

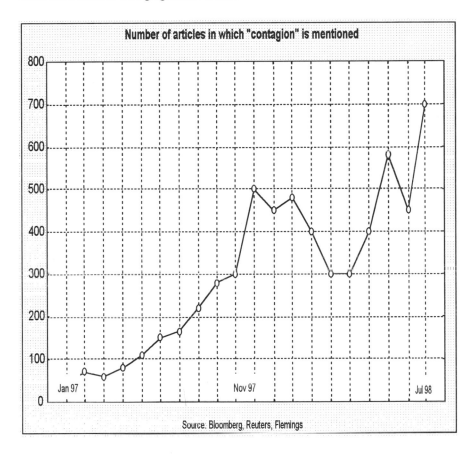

In conclusion of this book, the theory of memes adds a dimension of analysis to frontier emerging equity markets which creates the inimitable competitive advantage for a select few of frontier market portfolio managers. While the W-A-M approach and the dynamics of relative market efficiency, presented in the main parts of this book, open the door to exploiting pricing inefficiencies due to market segmentation, those frameworks can be adopted by the diligent student the discipline of frontier markets.

A thorough understanding of history and the philology of the frontier market valuation debate can only be acquired over time by those possessing a sharp sense of market history and a keen interest in the workings of the human mind. The separation of the winners from the losers in the exciting game of investment returns of uncharted equity markets is therefore decided by the skills which allow the portfolio managers to foresee and predict when the shape of the valuation debate – or for that matter the memetic valuation debate evolution- is suddenly transformed. To reap the rewards by seizing timely action, often requires a shrewd abandonment of the static rules of institutional asset management, and an intuitive understanding of the catalysts shifting the frontier market valuation debate in a more or a less favorable direction. Seeing the inflection point of the memetic valuation debate evolution in the frontier emerging market, therefore will become an increasingly valuable, and an increasingly indispensable tool in a market place where other informational advantages are eroding quickly, and where quantifiable insight is no longer a competitive advantage, but readily accessible to everyone in the investment community.

The frontier market equity environment will be increasingly dominated by trigger-happy and quick back-of-the-envelope analysis-driven macro hedge funds. This requires that lateral analysis of market segmentation theory and the disciplined and sensitive observation of the frontier market valuation debate must become daily tools for anyone dedicated to frontier markets. The full benefits are only achieved when used in more than just a casual manner.

Bibliography

Alexakis, Panayotis and Panayotis Petrakis. "Analysing Stock Market Behavior in Small Capital Markets." *Journal of Banking and Finance,* vol 15 (1991): 471-483.

Alexakis, Panayotis and Nicholas Apergis. "ARCH Effects and Cointegration: Is the Foreign Exchange Market Efficient?" *Journal of Banking and Finance,* vol 20 (1996): 687-697.

Alexander, S.S. "Price Movement in Speculative Markets: Trends of Random Walk." *Industrial Management Review* (1961): 7-26.

Aslund, Anders. *How Russia Became a Market Economy.* Washington, D.C.: The Brookings Institution, 1995.

Ayadi, O.F. and C.S. Pyun. "An Application of Variance Ratio Tests to the Korean Securities Market." *Journal of Banking and Finance,* vol 8 , issue 4 (September 1994): 643-658.

Bachelier, L. "Theory of Speculation." in Cootner P. (ed.), *The Random Character of Stock Market Prices.* Cambridge, MA: MIT Press, 1964; Reprint.

Bakaert, Geert; Claude Erb; Campbell R. Harvey; and Tadas Viskanta. "The Behavior of Emerging Markets Returns." in *The Future of Emerging of Emerging Market Capital Flows,* Edward Altman, Richard Levich, Jianping Mei, eds., forthcoming.

Bakaert, Geert, Campbell R. Harvey. "Speculators and Emerging Equity Markets." Working Paper, Duke University and Stanford University, 1996.

Ball R. and S.P. Kothari. "Non-stationary Expected Returns: Implications for Tests of Market Efficiency and Serial Correlation in Return." *Journal of Financial Economics,* vol 25 (1989): 51-74.

192

Bankers Trust Company. Corporate Trust & Agency Group— *Depository Receipts*

Bank of New York. *Global Offering of Depository Receipts-A Transaction Guide*

Bauman, W. Scott. "Channels Used to Research Global Equity Investments." *The Journal of Investing*, vol 5, no 4 (Winter 1996): 37-46.

Bernstein, Peter. *Capital Ideas*, New York, NY: The Free Press, 1993.

Black F. "Implications of the Random Walk Hypothesis for Portfolio Management." *Financial Analysts Journal*, vol 27 (1971) reprinted in Reilly (1975): 219-225.

Black, Fischer. "Noise." *The Journal of Finance*, vol 41 no 3 (1986): 529-543.

Bolen, D.W. and W.H. Boyd. "Gambling and the Gambler: A Review and Preliminary Findings." *Archives of General Psychiatry* 18, 5 (1968): 617-629.

Bobinski, Christopher. "Warsaw Begins to Recover," *Financial Times*, 22 April 1994, 37.

Brealey, Richard A. and Stewart C. Myers. *Principles of Corporate Finance*. 4th ed. New York, NY: McGraw-Hill, 1991.

Brenner, M. "The Effect of Model Misspecification on Tests of the Efficient Market Hypothesis." *Journal of Finance*, vol 32, no 1 (March 1977): 57-66.

Brunswick Brokerage. "Infrastructure Update." (February 19, 1997)

Brunswick Brokerage. "Russian Equity Guide." (1995)

Brunswick Brokerage. "Russian Equity Guide." (1996)

Butler, K.C. and S.J. Malaikah. "Efficiency and Inefficiency in Thinly Traded Stock Markets: Kuwait and Saudi Arabia." *Journal of Banking and Finance*, vol 16 (1992): 197-210.

Campbell, B. and J.M. Dufour. "Exact Non-Parametric Orthogonality and Random Walk Tests." *Review of Economics and Statistics*, vol 77 (February 1995): 1-16.

Chatfield C. *The Analysis of Time Series*. London: Chapman & Hall, 1996.

Christodoulakis, N.M. and S.C. Kalyvitis. "Efficiency Testing Revisited: A Foreign Exchange Market with Bayesian Learning." *Journal of International Money and Finance* vol 16, no 3 (1997): 367-385.

Claessens S.; S. Dasgupta and J. Glen. "Stock Price Behavior in Emerging Stock Markets." *World Bank Discussion Series on Emerging Stock Markets* (1996): chapter 13.

Cootner, P.H. "Stock Prices: Random vs. Systematic Changes." *Industrial Management Review*, vol 3 (Spring 1962): 24-45.

Corrado, Charles J. and Terry L. Zivney. "The Specification and Power of the sign Test in Event Study Hypothesis Tests Using Daily Stock Returns." *Journal of Financial and Quantitative Analysis* vol 27 no 3 (September 1992): 465-478.

Cottle, Sidney; Murray, Roger F. and Frank E. Block. *Graham and Dodd's Security Analysis.* 5th ed. New York, NY: McGraw-Hall, 1988.

Cowles, 3rd , Alfred. "Can Stock Market Forecaster Forecast?" *Econometrica*, vol 1 (July 1933): 309-324.

Daiwa Securities. "Central/Eastern Europe-Moving in Different Orbits." *Daiwa Europe Limited Equity Strategy Quarterly* (June 1997): 30.

Daniel, Kent and Sheridan Titman. "Evidence on the Characteristics of Cross Sectional Variation in Stock Returns." *Journal of Finance,* vol 52 no 1 (March 1997): 1-33.

Domowitz, Ian; Jack Glen; and Anath Madhavan. "Market Segmentation and Stock Prices: Evidence from and Emerging Market." *Journal of Finance*, vol 32, no 3 (July 1997): 1059-1085.

Durham, Brad. "Coming of Age." *The Russian* (July-August 1997): 24.

El-Erian, Mohamed A. and Mammohan S. Kumar. "Emerging Equity Markets in Middle Eastern Countries." *IMF Staff Papers* vol 32, no 2 (1995): 313-344.

Elton, E.J. and M.J. Gruber. *Modern Portfolio Theory and Investment Analysis.* New York: John Wiley and Sons, 1984.

Erb, Claude B.; Campbell R. Harvey; and Tadas E. Viskanta. "Political Risk, Economic Risk, and Financial Risk." *Financial Analyst Journal* forthcoming,1996b, also in http://www.duke.edu./~charvey/country_risk /coundix.htm.

Errunza, Vihang R. "Emerging Markets: Some New Concepts." *Journal of Portfolio Management* (Spring 1994): 82-87.

_____."Efficiency and the Programs to Develop Capital Markets." *Journal of Banking and Finance*, vol 3 (1979): 355-382.

Errunza, Vihang R. and E. Losq. "The Behavior of Stock Prices in LDC Markets." *Journal of Banking and Finance*, vol 9 (1985): 561-575.

Fama, E. "Efficient Capital Markets: A Review of Theory and Empirical Work." *Journal of Finance* (May 1970): 383-417.

_____."The Behavior of Stock Market Prices." *Journal of Business*, vol 38 (1965): 34-105.

_____."Random Walks in Stock Market Prices." *Financial Analysts Journal*, vol 51, issue 1 (Jan/Feb 1995): 75-80.

Fama, E. and M. Blume. "Filter Rules and Stock Market Trading Profits." *Journal of Business*, vol 39 (1966): 226-241.

Fama E. and K. French. "The Cross-Section of Expected Stock Returns." *Journal of Finance,* vol 47, no 2 (1992): 427-465.

_____."Multifactor Explanations of Asset Pricing Anomalies." *Journal of Finance* vol 51, no 1 (March 1996): 55-84.

Feldman, Robert A. and Mammohan S. Kumar. "Emerging Equity Markets: Growth, Benefits, and Policy Concerns." *World Bank Research Observer* (August 1995): 181-200.

Fisher, L. "Some New Stock-Market Indices." *Journal of Business.* (January 1966): 191-225.

194

Flemings Research. "Russia Coming in from the Cold." (August 1996)

Fluck, Z.; B.G. Malkiel, and R.E. Quandt. "The Predictability of Stock Returns: A Cross-Sectional Simulation." *The Review of Economics and Statistics* (March 1996): 176-183.

Fortune, Peter. "Stock Market Efficiency: An Autopsy?" *New England Economic Review-Federal Reserve Bank of Boston* (March/April 1991): 30-34.

Gordon Barry and Libby Rittenberg. "The Warsaw Stock Exchange: A Test of Market Efficiency." *Comparative Economic Studies,* vol 39, no. 2 (Summer 1995).

Gujarati D. N. *Basic Econometrics.* NY, NY: McGraw-Hill, 1995.

Giddy, Ian H. *Global Financial Market.* Lexington, MA: D.C. Heath and Company, 1994.

Hakim, Miquel "The Efficiency of the Mexican Stock Market." (Ph.D. diss., Claremont University, 1988).

Hamilton, J.D. *Time Series Analysis.* Princeton, NJ: Princeton University Press, 1994.

Hargis, Kent. "The Globalization of Trading and Issuance of Equities from Emerging Markets." *The Journal of Emerging Markets,* vol 2, no 1 (Spring 1997): 5-21.

Harvey, Campbell R. "Predictable Risks and Returns in Emerging Markets." *Review of Financial* Studies, vol 8 (1995): 773-816.

Harvey, Campbell R.; Andrew W. Lo ; and A. Craig MacKinlay. *The Econometrics of Financial Markets.* Princeton, NJ: Princeton University Press, 1997.

Haugen, R. *Modern Investment Theory.* Upper Saddle River, NJ: Prentice Hall, 1997.

Huang, B.N. "Do Asian Stock Markets Follow Random Walks? Evidence from the Variance Ratio Test." *Applied Financial Economics,* vol 5, issue 4 (August 1995): 51-256.

Jarque, M. and A.K. Bera. "A Test for Normality of Observations and Regression Residuals." *International Statistical Review*, vol 55 (1987): 163-172.

Jegadeesh, Narasimhanand, and Sheridan Titman. "Returns to Buying Winners and Selling Losers:Implications for Stock Market Efficiency." *Journal of Finance,* vol 48, no 1 (1993): 65-92.

Kelly, Morgan. "Do Noise Traders Influence Stock Prices?" *Money, Credit and Banking* (1991): 351-363.

Kennedy, Paul. *A Guide to Econometrics.* Cambridge, MA: The MIT Press, 1997.

King, B.F. "Market and Industry Factors in Stock Prices Behavior." *Journal of Business*, vol 39 (1966): 139-190.

Kramer, Charles. "Macroeconomic Seasonality and the January Effect." *Journal of Finance*, vol 49, no 5 (December 1994): 1883-1891.

La Porta, Rafael. "Expectations and the Cross-Section of Stock Returns." *Journal of Finance* vol 51, no 5 (December 1996): 1715-1742.

Leroy, S. "Risk Aversion and the Martingale Property of Stock Returns." *International Economic Review*, vol 14 (1973): 436-446.

Liu, C.Y. and J. He. "A Variance Ratio Test of Random Walks in Foreign Exchange Rates." *Journal of Finance*, vol 46, no 2 (1991): 773-785.

Lo, Andrew W. and A. Craig MacKinlay. "Stock Market Prices Do Not Follow Random Walks: Evidence from a Simple Specification Test." *The Review of Financial Studies*, vol 1, no 1 (1988): 41-66.

Lo, Andrew W. and A. Craig MacKinlay. "The Size and Power of the Variance-Ratio Test in Finite Samples: A Monte Carlo Investigation." Journal of Econometrics, vol 40 (1989): 203-238.

Lucas, R., Jr. "Asset Prices in an Exchange Economy." *Econometrica*, vol 46 (1978): 1429-1446.

Malkiel, Burton G. *A Random Walk Down Wall Street*. New York, NY: W.W. Norton & Company, 1991.

Markowitz, H.M. "Foundations of Portfolio Theory." *Journal of Finance*, vol 46, no 2 (June 1991): 469-477.

Mendelsohn, Morris and Junius W. Peake. "Equity Markets in Economies in Transition." *Journal of Banking and Finance*, vol 17 (1993): 913-929.

Mills, T.C. *The Econometric Modelling of Financial Time Series*. Cambridge, UK: Cambridge University Press, 1996.

Mitchell, Mark L. and Harold Mulherrin. "The Impact of Public Information on the Stock Market." *Journal of Finance*, vol 49, no 3 (July 1994): 923-949.

Morgan Stanley Dean Witter-Emerging Markets Investment Research. "Handle with Care: Selected Topics in Russian Accounting." (3 June 1997): 6-9.

Newbold, Paul. *Statistics for Business & Economics*. 4th ed. Englewood Cliffs, NJ: Prentice-Hall, 1994.

Ortiz, E. "Caminata al Azar en México: Importancia y Evidencia de la Bolsa Mexicana de Valores." *Contaduri y Administración* 104-105 (1980): 65-109.

Osborne, M.F.M. "Periodic Structure in the Brownian Movement of Stock Prices." *Operations Research*, vol 10 (May-June 1992): 245-279.

Park, K.K. and A.W. Van Agtmael. *The World's Emerging Stock Markets*. Chicago: Irwin Professional Publishing, 1993.

Pelaghias, Christodoulos. Seaward Intl., Cyprus, Harvard University Russia Conference, Jan. 9-11, 1998, Cambridge, Massachusetts, panel discussion.

Ray, M.; D. Thurston, and P. Dheeriya. "Effects of Seasoned Equity Issues in Emerging Markets: An Investigation in the Thai Stock Market." *The Journal of Emerging Markets*, vol 1, no 3 (Fall/Winter 1996): 22-34.

Reilly, F.K. *Investment Analysis and Portfolio Management.* Fort Worth, TX: The Dryden Press, 1989.

Richards, Anthony. "Volatility and Predictability in National Stock Markets. " *IMF Staff Papers*, vol 43, no 3 (September 1996): 461-501.

Schwaiger, Walter S.A. " A Note on GARCH Predictable Variances and Stock Market Efficiency." *Journal of Banking and Finance*, vol 19 (1995): 949-953.

Salomon Brothers, "Russian ADRs, Best Way to Enter the Russian Equity Market in 1997." (Jan 23 1997)

Salomon Brothers "Russian Equities Road Map-A Bullish View of the Bear." (September 1995).

Sawikin, Harvey. "The Russian Stock Market: First-Rank or Second-Rate?" *The Russian* (December/January 1998): 24-25.

Sias, Richard W. and Laura T. Starks. " Return Autocorrelation and Institutional Investors." *Journal of Financial Economics*, vol 46 (1997): 103-131.

Slater, M. "Take a Walk on the Random Side." *Investors Chronicle,* vol 107 (March 18, 1994): 12-13.

Shiller, Robert. "Human Behavior and the Efficiency of the Financial System." (www.econ.yale.edu/~shilller/handbook.html), 1997.

Shleifer, Andrei and Lawrence H. Summers. "The Noise Trader Approach in Finance." *Journal of Economic Perspectives* (Spring 1990): 19-33.

Stulz, Rene. "A Model of International Asset Pricing." *Journal of Financial Economics*, vol 9 (1981): 383-406.

Thaler, Richard, ed., *Advances in Behavioral Finance.* New York, NY: Russell Sage Foundation, 1993.

Urrutia, J.L. "Tests of Random Walk and Market Efficiency for Latin American Equity Markets." *Journal of Financial Research* (Fall 1995): 299-309.

Working, Holbrook. "A Random Difference Series for Analysis of Time Series." *Journal of the American Statistical Association*, vol 29 (March 1934):11-24.

Index